METTERNICH'S PROJECTS FOR REFORM IN AUSTRIA

METTERNICH'S PROJECTS FOR REFORM IN AUSTRIA

by

EGON RADVANY

MARTINUS NIJHOFF
THE HAGUE

1971

ISBN 978-94-011-8546-2 *ISBN 978-94-011-9302-3 (eBook)*
DOI 10.1007/978-94-011-9302-3

PREFACE

I would like to express my gratitude to the Graduate Center of the City University of New York for having received a summer grant for research in Austria.

I want to thank Dr. Franz Graf Meran for permitting me to use Archduke Johann's diaries and letters in the Steiermärkisches Landesarchiv, Graz, as well as Dr. Walter Puschnigg and the other gentlemen of that archive for their kind assistance.

I am also extremely grateful for the patient, friendly and unsparing helpfulness and advice from the ladies and gentlemen of the Haus-, Hof- und Staatsarchiv in Vienna. In particular I would like to thank w.Amtsrat Anton Nemeth for his aid in deciphering and transcribing numerous documents.

Finally, I am most grateful for the counsel, help and encouragement by Prof. Andrew Whiteside of Queens College and City University of New York, and for the many valuable suggestions made by Profs. Robert A. Kann of Rutgers University, Paula S. Fichtner and Bela K. Kiraly, both of Brooklyn College.

My wife Ruth deserves very special thanks for her patience, forbearance and proofreading.

TABLE OF CONTENTS

Ich weiss ein Land, das lag so unbeweglich,
Es regte kaum die Glieder wie ein Wurm,
In Ringen schob sich's nach der Nahrung täglich,
Die Zeit war nur ein Glockenschlag vom Turm;

Die nächste Nähe lag auf hundert Meilen,
Die Dämmerung gab noch zu helles Licht,
Das Höchste schien der Niedern Schmach zu teilen,
Und Ruhe war nicht bloss der Bürger Pflicht.

GRILLPARZER, "Vorzeichen".

INTRODUCTION

Metternich's Austria has been called "Joseph II's state, the welfare state" [1]. After the death of Emperor Leopold II in 1792, blind fear of revolution displaced much of the enlightened reason of eighteenth century Habsburg absolutism. In the name of law and order the imperial government opposed every form of change. The Josephinian concept of government for the people but not by the people degenerated into a police state, justified in the eyes of the rulers as necessary to preserve society. To Emperor Franz II – he becomes Franz I of Austria in 1804 – the constitution of society was indistinguishable from his own imperial and apostolic power [2].

Metternich did not, of course, create the system of absolutism. By the time Emperor Franz appointed him Foreign Minister in 1809, absolutism as understood in the eighteenth century was firmly established as a principle in which the monarch could legislate almost without any constitutional restraint, although as in all such despotisms he was bound by certain traditions. Emperor Franz returned to the centralism of his uncle, Joseph II, as a more efficient tool of imperial power than his father's, Leopold II's, incipient diversification. He lacked, however, Joseph II's intellectual grasp.

Metternich faced the old problem, dominant throughout Austrian history, of how to reconcile the one with the many, the unity of the state and the dynastic Reichsidee with the multiplicity of historic lands and national cultures. A solution of this problem became increasingly urgent in the first half of the nineteenth century due to growing national consciousness and aspirations, and to the decay of governmental institutions in an age of social and economic transformation. This situation was complicated during his early years as minister by the Napoleonic wars, defeats and loss of territory that reduced Austria to the status of a secondary power.

[1] Hugo Hantsch, *Die Geschichte Oesterreichs* (4th ed.; Graz: Styria, 1959), II, 288.

[2] Robert A. Kann, *A Study in Austrian intellectual History* (New York: Praeger, 1960), 271.

This work will deal with Metternich's attempts to create an efficient government by speeding up its decision making process and translating its results into effective action. He hoped to achieve these aims by a strict separation of governmental functions, particularly of policy making and administration, with the latter accommodating the cultural and historic diversity of the provinces. I am concerned only with that part of the Habsburg empire which was included in the German Confederation because Hungary, Galicia, the Bukovina and the Italian provinces, for historical and constitutional reasons, were either governed in a different manner or, when partially administered from Vienna, hardly affected the overall picture. Local, provincial or nationality questions are also outside the scope of this work.

CHAPTER I

THE AUSTRIAN GOVERNMENT

The Habsburg monarchy, an "agglomeration of territories ... and ... of nations" [1], as Metternich called it, had been accumulated through a conscious policy of marriages ever since Maximilian I had himself married the Burgundian heiress, his son to the Spanish and his grandson to the Bohemian-Hungarian princesses. Not until 200 years later, when the cohesive effect of the Turkish danger had disappeared, did the Habsburgs take any steps to unify the disparate possessions of the House of Austria. The Pactum Mutuae Successionis of 1703 and the Pragmatic Sanction of 1713 provided for "indivisible and inseparable" union and for succession through male and female lines [2].

In line with the general centralizing tendencies of the eighteenth century monarchies, Maria Theresia and her son Joseph II, her co-regent and successor, took a long step in the half century of their reigns towards concentrating all power in the hands of the monarch. The governors of the crownlands became explicitly representatives of the monarch, thus denying them any constitutional or organic connection with the provinces. Only Hungary and the Netherlands remained outside the scope of centralization (except for a brief period under Joseph II) but even in Hungary the centralizing trend gradually and informally undermined its ancient constitution.

Internally, new imperial institutions directed and supervised the administration of the provinces which had hitherto been partially the concern of the Estates, giving rise to the *Beamtenstaat* (bureaucratic state) and to the

[1] Richard von Metternich and Alfons von Klinkowström (eds.), *Aus Metternichs nachgelassenen Papieren* (Vienna: Braumüller, 1880-84) (hereafter cited as "*NP*"), VIII, 520.

[2] The Hungarian diet accepted the Pragmatic Sanction in 1722 but economically Hungary remained a separate unit until the middle of the nineteenth century.

uniquely Austrian constitutional problem of how to organize functionally and socially the central government and administration [3].

In 1809 the Austrian government was a conglomerate of three historical institutions: The *Hofstellen* (aulic departments), the *Staatsrat* (council of state) and the *Kabinett* (cabinet) [4]. These institutions cannot be reduced to a simple diagram because they had no consistent relationship to each other, no clear division of authority and responsibility, and only a very ambiguous place in the monarch's ultimate decisions. This basic situation formed the background to all of Metternich's activities in the internal sphere of the Habsburg empire.

The Hofstellen were administrative organs – analogous to the technical ministries in the Soviet Union today – whose function was to oversee the carrying out of executive orders. The chiefs of the Hofstellen were similar to the British permanent under-secretaries, that is, they were essentially heads of the civil service in their respective departments. In Metternich's day, with two exceptions, the executive of the Hofstellen was vested in a board headed by a president who was bound by majority decisions of his board.

The *Polizeihofstelle*, dealing with police and censorship matters, and the *Haus-*, *Hof- und Staatskanzlei* (House-, Court- and State-Chancellery), in charge of foreign affairs and the private business of the imperial house were always under the sole direction of one man. The other Hofstellen were the three chancelleries (*Hofkanzleien*), one each for Transylvania and Hungary, and one for the rest of the empire, the *Vereinigte Hofkanzlei*, which dealt with the administration of these regions; the *Hofkammer* which supervised financial and economic affairs; the *Hofrechenkammer* whose principal responsibility was government accounting; the *Hofkriegsrat*, essentially a war office; and the *Oberste Justizstelle* which combined the administration of justice with the function of a supreme court. All these institutions, the majority of which dated from the sixteenth century, had a somewhat chaotic history during which their names and functions changed [5].

[3] Joseph Redlich, *Das oesterreichische Staats- und Reichsproblem* (Leipzig: Der neue Geist Verlag, 1920), I/1, 25-30, 35.

[4] For the following see Friedrich Walter, *Die oesterreichische Zentralverwaltung, 1792-1848* (Vienna: Holzhausens Nf., 1956) hereafter cited as "Walter, *Zentralverwaltung*"; Franz von Hartig, *Genesis der Revolution in Oesterreich im Jahre 1848* (Leipzig: Fleischer, 1850), 26-45.

[5] See Alfons Huber, *Oesterreichische Reichsgeschichte* (Vienna: Tempsky, 1901), 196-310.

From the early sixteenth century onwards attempts were made to provide some council to advise the emperor on common policy affecting all provinces of his *Hausmacht* (dynastic possessions) as distinct from the affairs of the German Empire. A "*Geheimer Rat*" (secret council) of three to five high officials functioned well for about a hundred years but when the number of councillors had been inflated to about sixty, Leopold I appointed a few more important ones to the "*Geheime Conferenz*" (secret conference), a kind of cabinet usually presided over by the emperor. This conference disappeared early in the reign of Maria Theresia under the impact of war and reforms [6].

In 1760 Staatskanzler Prince Wenzel Kaunitz-Rittberg, in a letter to Empress Maria Theresia, took note of the growing evil of all branches of the government being administered ineffectively, without purpose, principles or system, often contradicting each other. As a solution he proposed an advisory council of men well acquainted with the situation in all provinces to assist Maria Theresia in dealing with internal affairs. This "Staatsrat", without executive power, was to control the Hofstellen and was to consist of three ministers, appointed from the nobility, and three *Staatsräte* (state-councillors) from the gentry. Kaunitz considered a Prime Minister to be unnecessary in view of the empress' diligence in government and, he added modestly, the difficulty of finding an appropriate person. Despite the urgency of war for a single direction of the government, Kaunitz seems to have been reluctant (if not too lazy) to take on more work and preferred a council which, under the circumstances, would give him the influence of a Prime Minister on internal affairs when and where he needed it [7]. In December 1760 Maria Theresia created the Staatsrat as proposed but only for the German-Bohemian provinces [8].

The Staatsrat did not meet to discuss the items on its agenda. Written opinions of each member were circulated on the basis of which one of the ministers drew up a draft for approval by the monarch. In case of disagreement the draft had to be recirculated. Since Joseph II was impatient with this cumbersome procedure the Staatsrat lost much influence during

[6] *Ibid.*, 196-98, 247.

[7] Friedrich Walter, *Die oesterreichische Zentralverwaltung, 1740-80* (Vienna: Holzhausens Nf., 1938), 269f. Kaunitz's letter printed in Friedrich Walter (ed.), *Die oesterreichische Zentralverwaltung, 1760-80, Aktenstücke*, (Vienna: Holzhausens Nf., 1934), 3-10.

[8] Carl Hock and Herman Bidermann, *Der oesterreichische Staatsrat, 1760-1848* (Vienna: Braumüller, 1879), 9-11.

his reign. In 1802 it was suspended by Emperor Franz [9] but restored in 1808.

To expedite the governmental process Joseph II enlarged and strengthened the insignificant cabinet which had served his mother as a private office. He drew its members from the Staatsrat and gave them a great deal of work and very little initiative or responsibility [10]. Franz, immediately upon his accession in 1792, appointed his tutor, Count Franz Colloredo-Walsee, Kabinettminister with extensive powers. By thus investing the Kabinett with an institutional character and with ample but undefined scope he provided the opportunity for an all-powerful minister to run the government. If Colloredo did not make use of it that was entirely due to the limitations of his ability and intellect [11]. He contended himself with supervising the government through the Staatsrat and through personal contact with heads of Hofstellen and Staatsräten. After his dismissal in 1805 as a result of Austerlitz [12], the Kabinett reverted to the unimportant position of the monarch's personal office while Emperor Franz tried to keep the strands of government together in his own hands by calling informally for opinions by experts dubbed "*Kabinettsreferenten*" (cabinet-reporters) and by substituting written reports for oral discussions [13].

The proliferation of central organs, some of them the debris of Joseph II's hasty improvisations, functioning without clear demarcation or unified purpose, was partly the result of Leopold's II restoration interrupted by his early death and the French wars, and of Emperor Franz's personality. Victor von Andrian-Werburg, a conservative nobleman, held "the poisonous plants of faulty and rotting institutions" responsible for the chaotic situation. His indictment of the *Vormärz* (pre-March) regime applies equally well to the position in 1809. The deadening effect of the educational process; the lack of incentive for able men, nobles or commoners; the ruinous influence of "the pernicious creeping plant" bureaucracy; the stifling centralization of "*zuvielregierenwollen*" (desire for excessive government) – all

[9] Until 1806, when Napoleon virtually abolished the Holy Roman Empire, Franz's title was "Franz II, Holy Roman Emperor". Two years earlier the hereditary monarchy of Austria was created in answer to Napoleon's French empire. Since 1804 Franz's title was "Franz I, Emperor of Austria".

[10] Walter, *Zentralverwaltung*, 34f.

[11] Ignaz Beidtel, *Geschichte der oesterreichischen Staatsverwaltung*, ed. Alfons Huber (Innsbruck: Wagner'sche Universitätsbuchhandlung, 1898), II, 21f.; Eduard Wertheimer, *Geschichte Oesterreichs und Ungarns im ersten Jahrzehnt des 19. Jahrhunderts* (Leipzig: Duncker & Humblot, 1884-90), I, 19.

[12] and pressure by Napoleon, according to Hartig (*Genesis*, 29).

[13] Walter, *Zentralverwaltung*, 50.

these were due not to the bureaucracy, nor to the aristocracy, nor even to the emperor, but to habit, to tradition, to "the irresistible power of routine" [14].

What then are the defects of the government machine "which revolves with tremendous noise yet can never move forward"? [15] To Kübeck [16] the institutions were "obsolete, frequently misunderstood and even more often misused for narrow purposes" [17]. He and other critics, contemporaries and historians, concentrated their fire on three problems: class distinction, procedures, and shortcomings of the emperor.

Kübeck deplored the vicious influence of the nobility, grasping all great offices of the state, "blocking the throne", thwarting anything that might threaten their feudal privileges and hating all officials who were more than "mere writing machines" [18]. He particularly attacked the position of the Hofstellenpräsidenten, usually aristocrats, vis-à-vis the members of their boards "from the middle class" or even lower classes who had been chosen for their ability (like Kübeck himself). These members, regarded by the presidents as *their* and not the emperor's councillors, did the actual work of the Hofstellen. Any councillor who acted independently and "had the misfortune" to contradict his president would be denounced by the latter to the emperor as a dangerous revolutionary, which meant, at least, the end of any influence or responsibility. The independence and truthfulness of the boards was thus gravely impaired; they became mere shields for the presidents' own purposes, protecting them from responsibility with majority votes. The Staatsrat was similarly "destroyed" by private interests of presidents who, if unable to obtain a majority vote from their boards, by-passed the Staatsrat under the pretext of urgency or secrecy to approach the monarch directly [19].

These accusations were simultaneously a stricture upon the board institution, a target of many other critics such as Andrian and Count Franz

[14] Victor von Andrian-Werburg, *Oesterreich und dessen Zukunft* (3rd ed. Hamburg: Hoffmann & Campe, 1843), 40-62, 147.

[15] Anton Springer, *Geschichte Oesterreichs seit dem Wiener Frieden 1809* (Leipzig: Hirzel, 1865), I, 120.

[16] Carl Friedrich von Kübeck, born in 1780 in Moravia as the son of a tailor, rapidly rose in the civil service through ability and force of character. Already a Hofrat at 32, he served as a Staatsrat from 1821 until 1840. He became president of the Hofkammer in 1840 and of the Reichsrat in 1851.

[17] Carl Friedrich von Kübeck, *Tagebücher des Carl Friedrich Freiherrn von Kübeck von Kübau*, ed. Max von Kübeck (Vienna: Gerold, 1909), I, 378.

[18] *Ibid.*, I, 333f.

[19] *Ibid.*, I, 379-81.

Hartig, a prominent member of the Staatsrat after 1840. They opposed it as denying individual responsibility, destroying initiative and causing delays by its written procedure. Oddly enough, Metternich, who insisted on conducting the Staatskanzlei as a ministry "guided by one will" [20], defended the board system in Hofstellen because, he argued, the advantages of orderly procedure and of a barrier to arbitrary action outweighed the disadvantages [21].

The *Hofcommissionen* (court commissions), appointed *ad hoc* to deal with any and every momentary difficulty, were also disliked because they achieved very little but tended to become permanent, thereby hampering regular authorities as well as wasting money and effort badly needed elsewhere [22].

But it was the emperor's own working habits and methods that the critics fastened upon most avidly. Already in 1792 Emperor Franz insisted upon hearing personally all contradictory opinions expressed by the *Referenten* (reporters) of the Hofkanzleien in order to know each one's "own strengths and weaknesses" [23]. From there, given the emperor's increasing distaste for discussions and conferences, it was only a short step to the notorious "*Kabinettweg*" (cabinet method) – the request for direct reports from individuals, often not even in official positions or very subordinate officials in remote districts [24]. Kübeck mildly deplored this advice from archdukes, ministers, lesser officials and others, mutually jealous and bitter about the limited extent of their influence but regarded as omnipotent by outsiders [25]. Metternich rejected the private reporting (*allein Referieren*) as "a source of great evil" because Emperor Franz, by his own admission, had often been misled into making bad decisions by partial advisers and the public had learned to blame all unpopular measures upon such misguidance [26]. Other bad results of the Kabinettweg were the reduction of

[20] *Vortrag* Metternich's, April 16, 1811, printed in Friedrich Walter (ed.), *Die oesterreichische Zentralverwaltung, 1792-1848, Aktenstücke* (Vienna: Holzhausens Nf., 1956) (hereafter cited as "*OZV*"), 182-207.

[21] Metternich to Archduke Ludwig, October 3, 1836, printed in Hanns Schlitter, *Aus Oesterreichs Vormärz* (Vienna: Amalthea Verlag, 1920), IV 94.

[22] Springer, *Geschichte*, I, 61.

[23] *OZV* 302.

[24] Springer, *Geschichte*, I, 112.

[25] Kübeck, *Tagebücher*, I, 209. Kübeck himself, as Staatsrat, frequently reported to the emperor.

[26] Metternich's Vortrag of 1811 (no date), "Allgemeine Betrachtungen über die gegenwärtige, und Vorschlag zu einer zweckmässigeren Zentralstaatsverwaltung", Haus-, Hof- und Staatsarchiv, Staatsrat Präsidium (Organisierung und Instruktionen), Fasz. III (hereafter cited as "HHSA, Praes."), Kart. 3.

Hofstellen to purely administrative functions, the decline of the Staatsrat starved of important questions, and the overburdening both of emperor and Hofstellen. In 1821 the Minister of Finance, Count Philipp Stadion, pleaded with Emperor Franz not to request "thousands of reports" utterly beyond the sphere of competence of the Hofstellen [27].

The emperor's "*Handbillets*" (notes), his answers to proposals or requests by the Hofstellen, expressed his decisions without reasons or explanations and were usually concerned with specific cases. They thus offered no guidance or principles to the officials to enable them to act in the spirit of Franz's intention. Indeed, collectively they were often contradictory, causing clashes within many departments with both sides able to base themselves on conflicting imperial orders. Hence misunderstandings, indifference, reluctance to take initiative and responsibility or to leave the well-trodden path of precedent and routine were prevalent. Similarly, the emperor's personal interference through Handbillets on behalf of high or low petitioners or informers undermined the authority of officials and tended to corrupt the bureaucracy by breeding a desire to guess imperial wishes and be "*nach oben gedeckt*" (protected against the superior) [28].

The result of the flood of opinions requested and submitted, rejected or returned for elucidation, sometimes through channels of five or six levels of bureaucracy controlling each other directly or through Hofcommissionen [29], and of frequently conflicting instructions, was endless delay. The government was "stationary", as Hartig put it, not from principle but from inability to come to a decision "with which foot to advance". Hence "the state was administered but not governed" [30].

It is not surprising, therefore, that Napoleon is supposed to have said: "Ces messieurs de Vienne sont toujours en retard d'une idée, d'une année, et d'une armée".

The chaotic nature of the government was thus largely due to "Franz's system which is called the Metternich system" based on the emperor's rejection of any limitation of his sovereign rights and personal power [31].

[27] Hartig, *Genesis*, 30f.; Walter, *Zentralverwaltung*, 139.

[28] Hartig, *Genesis*, 37ff.; Springer, *Geschichte*, I, 122f.; Victor Bibl, *Die niederoesterreichischen Stände im Vormärz* (Vienna: Gerlach & Wiedling, 1911), 9f.; Redlich, *Reichsproblem*, I/1, 165f.

[29] The Viennese called this "die controlirende [sic] Controle [sic] der controlirenden Controle". (Adolf Schmidt, *Zeitgenössige Geschichte* [Berlin: Dunker & Humblot, 1859], 480).

[30] Hartig, *Genesis*, 19, 45.

[31] *Ibid.*, 17, 43.

Kübeck accurately attributed as early as 1807 the "blurring and muddle" in the position and effectiveness of governmental organs diverted from their original purpose to "the personality and the will of the sovereign" [32], a sovereign, it must be stressed, to whom Kübeck was profoundly grateful and whose memory he honored all his life.

[32] Kübeck, *Tagebücher*, I, 208.

CHAPTER II

SOVEREIGN AND SERVANT

Franz's biographers like to contrast him with his uncle, Joseph II, emphasizing their changed roles, with the older man dynamic, full of lively, youthful impatience and the young prince slow and deliberate, with "the heart of an old man" [1]. In 1784 Joseph brought his 17 year old nephew – eldest son of Leopold, Grand Duke of Toscana – to Vienna from his native Florence in order to supervise his education. Later that year he wrote a report for the guidance of Franz's tutors. He found in the prince's "thinking, doing and leaving undone an immeasurable love of self, indolence, indifference and indecision" [2]. Much of this remained with him all his life.

Joseph also complained that Franz persisted in "esteeming with misplaced pride" his high birth instead of human values [3]. Later, as emperor, Franz regarded himself "God's substitute (*Statthalter*) on earth ... with a divine mission to preserve peace and order" [4], in the judgment of one of his officials, a liberal opponent. He had a patriarchal concept of his empire as a family entail to be ruled firmly and well. He considered crimes against the state as personal insults to be treated as lèse-majesté [5]. In 1813 he crossed out the word "Vaterland" in the War Manifesto and replaced it by "Kaiser" [6]. Six years earlier a change in the official ranking had reversed

[1] Cölestin Wolfsgruber, *Franz I, Kaiser von Oesterreich* (Vienna: Braumüller, 1899), II, 12; Walter Langsam, *Francis the Good* (New York: Macmillan, 1949), 56.

[2] Langsam, *Francis*, 60.

[3] Springer, *Geschichte*, I, 54; Victor Bibl, *Der Zerfall Oesterreichs* (Vienna: Rikola, 1922-24), I, 54.

[4] Eduard Castle, "Aus dem Tagebuch des Freiherrn Max von Löwenthal", *Historische Blätter*, I (1921/23), 496.

[5] Heinrich von Srbik, *Metternich: Der Staatsmann und der Mensch* (3rd ed. Munich: Bruckmann, 1957), I, 446f.

[6] Redlich, *Reichsproblem*, I/1, 54.

the positions of state and court. The "allerhöchste Hof" now took precedence over the state. A colleague's remarks to Kübeck summed up the situation succinctly:

> Emperor Joseph recognized the state as the purpose, and the welfare of the people as the aim of his high position, and himself as the highest official of the empire. ... The new form of schema restores the sovereign as the purpose, the court-nobility as partners and the state as a means [7].

There can be no doubt about Emperor Franz's good qualities, attested to by his contemporaries. He lived and dressed modestly, walked without guards in the streets, was accessible to all, even the humblest. He was hardworking, conscientious, charitable [8]. Adam Müller admired his "strict observance of juridical forms", which Metternich, less kindly, called "a sense of legality (of the inviolability of laws) exaggerated to the point of timidity" [9].

The emperor was, in fact, narrowminded and petty, insisting on traditional forms, and reluctant to come to a decision. As Metternich delicately phrased it, "it was his narrow conscience that prevented him from acting forcefully". Hence he always found it difficult to "deviate from a norm, not in principle ... but in form" [10]. Where Joseph II saw the problems of government in the context of principles and ideas, Franz, sedulously occupied with his sole purpose of preserving absolutism, was unable and unwilling to see issues in the light of ideas – even conservative ones. He only attended pragmatically to the facts of each case and thus failed to provide general guidance or policy [11]. Time only made matters worse, as Friedrich von Gentz remarked in 1830: "The only aim of the empress is to preserve the emperor's life. She therefore keeps every intellectual effort off him" [12].

Lack of self-confidence was the basic flaw in the emperor's character and many other defects were rooted in it. Hartig traced it back to the effect of Joseph II's outspoken impatience with his slow and unimaginative mind [13]. The uncle lamented that only Franz's "dread of vexations" could

[7] Kübeck, *Tagebücher*, I, 206f.

[8] Louis de Sainte-Aulaire, *Souvenirs* (Vienne, 1832-41) (Paris: Calmann-Lévy, 1926), 35; Adam Müller, *Gesammelte Schriften* (Munich: Franz, 1839), 380.

[9] Müller, *Schriften*, 388; *NP*, III, 8.

[10] Metternich to Kübeck, May 1, 1842, printed in Adolf Beer, "Kübeck und Metternich", *Denkschriften der kaiserlichen Akademie der Wissenschaften*, XLV (1897), 29.

[11] Kann, *Intellectual History*, 280ff.

[12] Anton Prokesch von Osten, *Aus den Tagebüchern 1830-34* (Vienna: C. Reissers Söhne, 1909), 29.

[13] Srbik, *Metternich*, I, 447f.; Hartig, *Genesis*, 18.

arouse this "spoiled mother's son" from his "sulkiness" but that this produced only short-lived efforts and promises without altering his wrong-headed attitudes [14]. Almost forty years later, Kübeck found that Emperor Franz became angry when contradicted and even angrier when one apologized for the contradiction and thus made clear that he could not tolerate it [15].

Given this diffidence, the emperor naturally preferred mediocrities to strong and able men who might seize the reins of government from him. "No good will come of geniuses and scholars", he said, "they always know better ... sound common sense and honest perseverance (*brav Sitzfleisch*) are best". And the professors of the Ljubljana Lyceum were told bluntly, "I do not need scholars but good citizens" [16]. The historian Anton Springer (born in 1825) asserted that a sure path to imperial favor and political influence was the ability to cut out silhouettes or make transparencies and dolls' carriages [17]. Archduke Johann regretted this temporary influence of various people and called his brother "changeable like April weather" [18]. No wonder, Count Kolowrat-Liebsteinsky complained to Kübeck that anybody who had to serve in the emperor's immediate surroundings had to be "either a philosopher, or an intriguer or a beast, in order to put up with it". Kübeck thought intriguer to be the *juste milieu* [19].

Emperor Franz's lack of self-confidence bred an "all-pervasive mistrust". Even his brothers suffered from this and from his exalted belief in the dignity of his position which precluded all close and intimate relations [20]. The popularity and intellectual superiority of Carl, the victor of Aspern, of Johann and Joseph, as well as the espousal of popular causes by the first two – all fed the emperor's distrust [21]. He was suspicious of Carl ever since Napoleon had proposed to depose Franz and replace him by Carl in 1809. The Palatine Joseph was suspected of wanting to separate Hungary from the empire, while Johann had lost his brother's favor in 1813 when he had tried to provoke an Alpine uprising against Napoleon [22]. Metternich

[14] Springer, *Geschichte*, I, 110; Wolfsgruber, *Franz*, II, 25.

[15] Kübeck, *Tagebücher*, I, 653.

[16] Bibl, *Zerfall*, I, 197; Springer, *Geschichte*, I, 119.

[17] Springer, *Geschichte*, I, 113.

[18] Berthold Sutter, "Erzherzog Johanns Kritik an Oesterreich", *Mitteilungen des oesterreichischen Staatsarchivs*, XVI (1963), 174.

[19] Kübeck, *Tagebücher*, I, 533.

[20] "Et suspicio caro facta est", Kübeck noted (*ibid.*, 552). Kolowrat called Franz: "personified mistrust" (*ibid.*, 316).

[21] Springer, *Geschichte*, I, 116f.

[22] Kübeck, *Tagebücher*, I, 564; Ludwig Frankl, *Erinnerungen* (Prague: Josef Koch,

contributed to this mistrust, particularly during the days of his unpopular French alliance in 1812, by describing the three archdukes in secret police reports as intriguers and plotters [23].

Lack of self-confidence and distrust produced a petit-bourgeois bureaucratism above which Emperor Franz never managed, or indeed cared, to rise. Metternich used to joke that the emperor worked his way through a bundle of state-papers like a red tapeworm until he emerged without having done more than make a hole in the documents. Franz said of himself he might have become a good Hofrat [24]. He was happiest sitting at his desk for hours, working on thousands of requests for pensions and promotions or permissions to turn an acre of forest into farmland – all questions reserved for his personal decision. Each begging letter seems to have been handled six times by the emperor before being finally granted or refused [25].

His brothers deplored this inability to delegate authority. Johann who loved him like a father – Emperor Franz had helped to bring up his brothers after Leopold's II early death – saw the situation clearly in 1811:

> The trouble is the emperor does everything by himself, asks and trusts nobody; from all the advice he gets something is patched together which ... is quite unsuitable [26].

Carl urged that the man charged with guiding an enterprise should expound principles and leave their execution to persons he could trust. He likened the emperor to "a coachman who loses his freedom to steer by trying to pull the carriage" [27]. Both archdukes hoped all their lives – in vain – to obtain a position of trust and responsibility from their brother or his successor. Metternich, who did obtain such a position, also regretted that Emperor Franz took on too much, thereby "smothering himself" and bringing business to a standstill. Many questions of the highest importance, he pointed out after Franz's death, had been dealt with "at the worst

1910), 149. In Carl's case what Gordon Craig has called the "Wallenstein complex" – the suspicion of great field commanders – contributed to the mistrust (Gordon A. Craig, *War, Politics and Diplomacy* [New York: Praeger, 1966], 5).

[23] Srbik, *Metternich*, I, 143f.; Joseph von Hammer-Purgstall, *Erinnerungen aus meinem Leben 1774-1852* (Vienna: Hölder-Pichler-Temsky, 1940), 230. On Metternich's relations with the archdukes, see chapter XV below.

[24] Adam Wandruszka, *The House of Habsburg* (New York: Anchor Books, 1964), 137f.; Kübeck, *Tagebücher*, I, 659; Hartig, *Genesis*, 15.

[25] Hartig, *Genesis*, 34; Castle, "Tagebuch Löwenthals", 505.

[26] Sutter, "Johanns Kritik", 174.

[27] Erzherzog Carl, *Ausgewählte Schriften*, ed. [F.X. Malcher] (Vienna: Braumüller, 1894), VI, 533.

moment, the eve of necessity" [28]. The trouble, of course, was that the emperor loathed making decisions. "One has to sleep on this", was his favorite saying [29]; and sometimes he slept for years.

Emperor Franz's pedantic mind saw in the government only a mechanism. His aim was, in his own words, to organize the government in such a way "that the entire administration will run on like a well constructed clockwork once it has been started up properly" [30]. Already as crown prince, in 1791, in a memorandum on the defects of the government, he attributed the "sad situation" to the laziness and selfishness of the officials servicing "the machine". There was no adverse criticism of the institutions themselves, their structure or organization [31].

Having set up an appropriate machine, there was no need for any changes. "I do not want any reforms", Emperor Franz told Staatsrat Pillersdorf who had apologized in advance for any changes that might seem opportune at the Hofkanzlei whose chancellor he had just become. "One should apply the laws justly. Our laws are good and adequate. Justice is all that matters". He regretted the few changes that had been made and always found excuses to refuse others. "Now is no time for reforms", he said in 1831, "my peoples are as if badly injured" [32]. To the Russian minister he explained: "My empire is like a dilapidated building. If you want to demolish a part of it, you do not know how much you might cause to collapse" [33].

Thus Austria's constitutional problems to a large extent resolved themselves into the question of how to reduce the work-load of the monarch deriving from his all-embracing power of decision while maintaining the principle of absolutism. All experiments failed in the end because Emperor Franz insisted on controls which defeated the aim of a measure of decentralization without really granting him the assurance of firm overall direction. After Colloredo's fall only one man received a great deal of confidence for having saved the emperor from a desperate situation but even that was not enough to allow a thorough reform of the government. It merely confirmed the special position of foreign policy and the Staatskanzlei [34].

[28] Metternich to Archduke Ludwig, December 3, 1836, HHSA, Staatskanzlei, Personalia, Metternich, Fasz. 12 (hereafter cited as "P.M.").

[29] Springer, *Geschichte*, I, 437.

[30] Handschreiben, August 31, 1801, printed in *OZV*, 100.

[31] Wolfsgruber, *Franz*, II, 198-201; Victor Bibl, *Kaiser Franz* (Leipzig: Günther, 1938), 21.

[32] Kübeck, *Tagebücher*, I, 438f. "Who injured them?" Kübeck asked in parentheses.

[33] Peter Meyendorff, "Portraits", *Baltische Monatsschrift*, LXX, Band 11 (1910), 295; cf. Srbik, *Metternich*, I, 449.

[34] Walter, *Zentralverwaltung*, 32, 213.

Count Clemens Lothar Metternich was born in 1773 in Coblenz in the Rhineland to an old *reichsunmittelbare* (direct subject of the emperor) noble family. Educated at the University of Strassburg, he married the grand-daughter of Staatskanzler Kaunitz in 1795. Six years later he entered the imperial diplomatic service. After serving as envoy in Dresden, Berlin and Paris, he was appointed Foreign Minister in 1809.

The confidence Emperor Franz reposed in Metternich was by no means based on a similarity of personality or politics. If the emperor was narrow-minded, absolutist, stubbornly unyielding with a hostility to change amounting to a mania, Metternich was sagacious, conservative, pragmatic and flexible. "A statesman must not be an iron bar", he liked to say, "but rather a steel spring which yields to every pressure but also resists it, and, as soon as it ceases, resumes its former shape" [35].

"It is impossible not to be personally devoted to the emperor", Metternich wrote to his father in 1809. Ten years later, in letters to his son Victor, he called Emperor Franz, only five years his senior, "his surest guide and most tender father", as well as his "best friend in the world". Franz told Victor that "he owed his throne, the monarchy its well-being and Europe its peace" to his father [36].

Their relationship was not an easy one. Metternich could never fully rely on his monarch, still less take him for granted. In 1818 he proudly wrote to Countess Lieven, his new mistress, "the emperor always does what I want but I never want anything but that which he has to do. He is convinced of that ..." [37]. Later he modified that boast: "Heaven has placed me next to a man who might have been created for me, as I for him. The Emperor Franz ... knows what he wants and that never differs in any way from what I must want" [38]. Soon he admitted that he was the only man who knew what he wanted and, "moreover, who could judge what he was able to want in view of his master" [39].

He knew how to handle his monarch. Writing to Lieven about a conversation with the emperor on a proposed journey that Metternich wanted

[35] Quoted by his physician, Dr. F. Jäger, in Frankl, *Erinnerungen*, 231f. The trouble with Dr. Jäger's memoirs is that they are second hand. Frankl, a physician and a poet, recorded Metternich's words as Jäger remembered them after many years.

[36] Quoted in Egon Cäsar Corti, *Metternich und die Frauen* (Zurich-Vienna: Europa Verlag, 1948), I, 195; *NP*, IV, 533, 338; Victor's letter in Corti, *Metternich*, II, 211.

[37] *Lettres du Prince de Metternich à la Comtesse de Lieven 1818-19*, ed. Jean Hanoteau (Paris: Libraire Plon, 1909), 71.

[38] Metternich to Lieven, July 17, 1820, printed in Corti, *Metternich*, II, 132f.

[39] Metternich to Lieven, November 16, 1920, printed *ibid.*, II, 147.

them to undertake soon, he described how – in the face of Franz's indecicion – he had argued for postponement, and added gleefully: "... and do you know, mon amie, what will happen? We shall depart. Thus everything proceeds according to my will" [40]. Yet there were limits and Metternich was undoubtedly nearest the truth when he told a Russian general,

> [Franz's] will is strong and nobody can persuade him to do what he does not want. If he overwhelms me with kindness and has confidence in me, it is because I walk in the path he has laid down for me. Had I the misfortune to diverge from it, Prince Metternich would not remain Foreign Minister for twenty-four hours [41].

One might therefore agree with Peter von Meyendorff, the Russian minister in Vienna, that "Austrian politics is based on Franz's character and guided by Metternich's spirit" [42].

Explaining his personality to Countess Lieven, Metternich stressed that he had conquered innumerable opponents through sang-froid, fearless action and, above all, "plain, simple reason" [43]. Although he liked to describe himself as a man of action, even speaking of his love for battlefields and cannon-shots [44], it would be more accurate to class him as a man of thought who seemed to prefer reasoning about things to experiencing them [45]. "I reason about everything and on every occasion", he wrote to Lieven [46]. As a child of the century of Enlightenment, he declared "the simple voice of reason" to be his "secret" and expressed "his hatred of the romantic, the unclear, the inferior". "My temperament is a *historical* one", he stressed, "opposed to every kind of *romanticism*" [47].

"I am above all a man of principles", he wrote in 1843 [48]. His enemies denied this. Hofrat Josef von Hammer, orientalist and chief interpreter for the Staatskanzlei, told Kübeck that Metternich despite his constant talk of principles had none. The press, with which he was continuously quarreling, influenced greatly "his daily mood which, at bottom, determines his measures" [49]. What his enemies did allow him was "the Metternich

[40] *Lettres Metternich à Lieven*, 94.

[41] Quoted in Srbik, *Metternich*, I, 453f.

[42] Meyendorff, "Portraits", 298.

[43] *Lettres Metternich à Lieven*, 256f.

[44] Srbik, *Metternich*, I, 256.

[45] *Ibid.*, 259; Martin Spahn, "Metternich", *Hochland*, 6. Jahrgang, II (1909), 166f.

[46] *Lettres Metternich à Lieven*, 129.

[47] *NP*, VI, 513; III, 440; Prokesch, *Tagebücher*, 225; *NP*, VII, 635.

[48] Friedrich Walter, "Metternich und Gervay, ein Briefwechsel", *Mitteilungen des oesterreichischen Staatsarchivs*, IX (1956), 254.

[49] Kübeck, *Tagebücher*, I, 381.

system" which they identified with absolutism, police and censorship. Metternich indignantly denied its existence. "An empty sound", "a shibboleth", he called it, and maintained that it was "not a system but a *Weltordnung*", "the foundation of social life" [50]. But while he disowned his system and generally believed "preconceived systems" to be fruitless, he distinguished between them and principles. He found the latter to be indispensable but thought that they achieved real value only through application [51].

It is, therefore, important for an understanding of Metternich's policies to consider some of the principles upon which they were based. He claimed, with much justification, that they did not change throughout his life. "My principles, my dear Prince, have not changed and they will never change", he wrote to the Bavarian minister Karl Wrede [52]; and to Lieven: "At fifteen I was what I am at forty-five ... in twenty years [the same]". And again: "the best moral element in me is immutability" [53]. But one must also keep in mind that he wrote to Kübeck, in 1845, "the foundation for everything ... is based on the only useful supports of principles and experience" [54]. Over the years experience, if it did not modify his principles, at least affected their application. Srbik, who disagrees with Metternich's "sophistry" in distinguishing system and principles [55], has provided an admirable analysis of his assumptions and political thinking [56] even if, as one critic rightly observed, it presents Metternich as too systematic a philosopher while he was only "a strongly systematizing and theorizing statesman" [57].

In the spirit of eighteenth century philosophy, Metternich looked for law and order by deductive method in nature, in society and in the state. Believing in the dualism of moral and material worlds, of the elements of positive conservation and negative destruction, of order and anarchy,

[50] *NP*, VII, 622, 628; VII, 200, 517; *Metternich und Kübeck, ein Briefwechsel*, ed. Max von Kübeck (Vienna: Gerold, 1910), 39.

[51] *NP*, VII, 634, 639; VI, 339; III, 416.

[52] Victor Bibl, *Metternich in neuer Beleuchtung* (Vienna: Seidel, 1928), 221.

[53] *Lettres Metternich à Lieven*, 257, 76.

[54] *Metternich-Kübeck, Briefwechsel*, 31.

[55] Srbik, *Metternich*, I, 322.

[56] *Ibid.*, 350-414. His "Der Ideengehalt des Metternichschen Systems", *Historische Zeitschrift*, CXXXI (1925), 240-62, is essentially an abbreviation of this analysis.

[57] E. Kittel, "Metternich's politische Grundanschauungen", *Historische Vierteljahrschrift*, XXIV (1927), 447. In his own essay, however, while differently organized, Kittel reaches similar conclusions with similar effect.

of repose and excessive movement, "forever at war with one another" [58], his system is an expression of the reaction (in the scientific, not the political, sense) to the revolution, of a counter-move to restore the "balance" he equated with the "health" of society [59]. Balance was as essential to society as to international relations. Internal social and political peace was secured by balancing the restless and destructive middle class with the conservative forces of a powerful nobility and the materially contented masses. It was the function of the nobility to mediate the dualism of crown and masses, to prevent a dangerous confrontation between them [60].

The alternative to popular sovereignty with its tendency to disorder, destruction and anarchy [61] is "pure monarchy", without concessions to constitutional forms. This does not mean, however, a monarchic despotism – "despotism of any kind is a sympton of weakness" – but a "monarchie temperée", limited by the laws of a moral worldorder [62]. A council is necessary to guide the monarch, to curb any arbitrariness and to preserve public and private rights.

While no compromise with eternal principles is possible, adjustments within their limits are permissible and sometimes even essential. "Stability", he wrote to Alexander I, "does not mean immobility", and thirty years later he stressed to Kübeck that "conservatism is based on active policy". Hence laws and rules must be adapted to the needs of the time. A statesman, in short, must be firm and flexible at the same time and must modify principles, without sacrificing them, according to difficult situations [63]. "*La force des choses*", "*die Gewalt der Dinge*" – to use a favorite phrase of his [64] – is on occasion so strong that one must submit and even violate one's principles. In that case, says the realist, one must provide a sanction of law for illegal changes. One must take the situation without illusion or complaint and wait until the chaotic phase in the cycle of society has run its course.

[58] *NP* VII, 636.

[59] *NP*, VIII, 549f.

[60] *NP*, VIII, 548.

[61] In Austria, he argued, it would lead to the dissolution of the empire into its many parts (*NP*, III, 174f.; VIII, 465).

[62] *NP*, VII, 634; III, 457. "The emperor of Austria is no absolute ruler", he wrote to Wrede (Bibl, *Neue Beleuchtung*, 249).

[63] *NP*, III, 415; VIII, 288; VII, 140; V, 320. Kübeck noted tersely how Metternich, during a discussion of rail-road matters, abandoned his "correct principles as soon as he had to apply them" to a specific case (*Tagebücher*, I, 771).

[64] *NP*, V, 135; VII, 605; VIII, 492.

This philosophy of flexible conservative realism was very different from the Catholic dogmatism of an Adam Müller or similar romantic writers. It was, as Robert Kann demonstrates, the resultant of the influence of enlightened absolutism, conservatism and romanticism [65]. Srbik calls it "the politics of perseverance and conservation" and finds its basis in Metternich's personal inclination towards repose. He misses in it a strong, active, dynamic element [66], a judgment that might almost as well be applied to Metternich's character.

[65] Kann, *Intellectual History*, 268-71.

[66] Srbik, "Ideengehalt", 243, 261.

CHAPTER III

REFORM BEFORE METTERNICH

The first five years of Emperor Franz's reign were a period of erratic experiments intended to improve the cumbersome governmental machine. While the Hofstellen were also involved [1], the principal efforts concentrated on the Staatsrat. The number of ministers and Staatsräte was first decreased and then increased; parts of the Hofrechenkammer were added to the Staatsrat and removed again within a year; there were four organizational changes concerned with the vexed question of whether or not to divide the work of the Staatsrat according to subject or provinces or both or none.

Few of these measures had any lasting beneficial effect. In 1797, taking advantage of the emperor's favor, Count Franz Saurau, governor of Lower Austria, delivered a scathing attack on governmental institutions, especially the Staatsrat, and on its senile, selfish or unfit members [2]. He particularly denounced its agenda containing thousands of trivial items, its lack of discussion and regular sessions. Instead of the Staatsrat he proposed "three able assistants" to the emperor, responsible for military, internal and Hungarian affairs. This was the first shot in a campaign that was to last some twenty-five years, and it was totally unsuccessful.

The next attack was the strongest, most comprehensive and – temporarily – most effective of the pre-Metternich era. Soon after the Treaty of Luneville which in February 1801 had virtually destroyed the Holy Roman Empire and given Austria Venetia in exchange for the Netherlands, the emperor decided on a reorganization of the government. He invited his brother Carl, the victor of Stockach and Zürich, to submit his ideas. The archduke, in a long and closely reasoned report [3], roundly condemned the

[1] Mainly through the combination of Hofkammer and Vereinigte Hofkanzlei into a "*Directorium*".

[2] Vortrag Saurau's, May 16, 1797, printed in *OZV*, 53-70. The attack did not hurt him; he was soon promoted to Hofkammerpräsident.

[3] Vortrag Carl's, July 24, 1801, extracts printed *ibid.*, 77-87.

Staatsrat. By excluding all foreign and military affairs – both intimately bound up with financial and other internal matters – and by having sunk to the level of a mere organ of revision for the Hofstellen instead of being the central juncture of the entire government, the Staatsrat had degenerated into "empty, dead" routine. It should be replaced, urged Archduke Carl, by a "*Konferenzministerium*" divided into three departments – war and navy, foreign, and internal affairs – each headed by a minister. The ministers, meeting twice a week for deliberation, were to determine policy and report only on the most important matters to the emperor on whom their advice was not binding. Their first task was to define their exact sphere of competence as well as those of the Konferenzräte, Hofstellen and provincial institutions, thus ending the perennial jurisdictional disputes and overlapping responsibilities.

Carl thus advocated two crucial innovations. First, the new Konferenzministers, unlike the Staatsministers of the Staatsrat, were to be part of the executive. Second, government and administration were to be separated: while the chiefs of the Hofstellen were to be responsible for the details of the latter and for each of their board members (this was a clear rejection of the direction of Hofstellen by boards), the ministers were charged with policy making, the "thinking (*meditirend*) part of the business", and – through the *Ministerrat* (council of ministers) – the general survey of the government [4].

Emperor Franz accepted these proposals and issued instructions in August 1801 to abolish the Staatsrat and organize a Staats- und Konferenzministerium with Carl as Minister of War in addition to his current presidency of the Hofkriegsrat. The emperor soon, however, fell under the influence of the war party which obstructed Carl and his reforms of the military administration, and intrigued against his opposition to a renewed war he thought Austria could not win. Within three years Franz deprived his brother of the Hofkriegsrat presidency and of much of his influence as War Minister, until the catastrophies of Austerlitz and the Peace of Pressburg restored Carl's prestige and his presidency [5].

Even worse, the rest of the reforms were never implemented. Negotiations on the organization of the ministry of the interior dragged on for more than a year and the final result resembled the old Staatsrat not only in its structure and written procedure but also in its name: "*Staatsrat in inneren Angelegenheiten*". The Ministerrat never really functioned because the

[4] This decisive difference between ministers and chiefs of Hofstellen was elaborated in a later memorandum (Walter, *Zentralverwaltung*, 243).

[5] Walter, *Zentralverwaltung*, 302-16.

emperor who presided and most of the members disliked discussion and soon returned to written reports and alleinreferieren [6].

By 1806 Carl's enemies, ministers and other high officials, had succeeded in wrecking his Konferenzministerium in all but name, not least by arousing Emperor Franz's mistrust and jealousy [7]. Konferenzminister Count Karl Zinzendorf and Staatsrat Anton von Baldacci urged an immediate return to the Staatsrat. The latter's voluminous memorandum [8] included innumerable suggestions for improvements of the Staatsrat designed to relieve the emperor of his excessive work-load and to "reassure" him – Baldacci shared Franz's distrust of officials – that his orders were really followed. Thus at least two Staatsräte were to report on each item; in case of disagreement several more had to report and the documents were "recirculated"; Staatsräte were to undertake journeys of inspection into the provinces.

The emperor accepted many of these proposals in the instructions he issued in 1807 for the new Interior Department [9] without, of course, accelerating its routine. Carl's appeal for a strong ministry to ensure the future of the state in case of Emperor Franz's sudden death (the heir to the throne, Archduke Ferdinand, was only fifteen, and there were already doubts about his mental and physical fitness) could only strenghten the emperor's distrust despite his awareness of the government's grave defects.

Hence Franz resorted to his old device of calling for ever more advice. The first one to offer it was Archduke Johann, in February 1807. He had no use for the old Staatsrat, that "pit in which everything got stuck". He wanted a new council of ministers and archdukes to advise the monarch on all important business; this would leave him free time "to think and read useful books in order to keep up with the spirit of the time ..." [10]. His true opinion of the situation he confided to his diary.

> The sovereign at the head has taken everything onto himself. Jealous of his power, he allows insight to nobody; everything comes to a stop – no decision – nothing but contradictions. He does not, or does not want to, understand the situation and thus leads his state irretrievably towards destruction [11].

[6] *Ibid.*, 90f.

[7] *Ibid.*, 82-97; Wertheimer, *Geschichte*, I, 86-106; Springer, *Geschichte*, I, 60-63.

[8] Printed in *OZV*, 497-633.

[9] "Instruktion für den Staats- und Konferenzrat", January 4, 1807, printed in *OZV*, 149-63.

[10] Franz von Krones, *Zur Geschichte Oesterreichs im Zeitalter der französischen Kriege und der Restauration, 1792-1816* (Gotha: Perthes, 1886), 69-74. It is not clear whether Johann was asked for his opinion or offered it on his own initiative.

[11] Erzherzog Johann's Tagebücher, November 23, 1810, unpublished, in the Steiermärkisches Landesarchiv, Graz.

Saurau was the first of the ministers to report to Emperor Franz [12]. As critical now of the Staatsrat – whose restoration was imminent – as he had been eleven years ago, he was equally forthright on the emperor's own "not rare" contribution to retard the government; he had, however, few positive ideas for reform. Count Philipp Stadion, the Foreign Minister, thought Carl's reforms to be on the right path, while Count Carl Zichy expressed his satisfaction with the situation [13]. The only useful contribution came from Archduke Rainer, one of the emperor's youngest brothers. His indictment of the government included "lack of system, delay, indecision, feebleness, half-measures, partiality, great immorality of officials", with "alleinreferieren" as the main cause of trouble.

In the mid-nineties Emperor Franz had instituted small irregular conferences to resolve disagreements in the Staatsrat, but he had quickly abandoned them in his insurmountable aversion to oral deliberation. Rainer now proposed in their place a weekly "grosse Conferenz" of a small permanent body of Staatsrat members "ad deliberandum et finaliter concludendum" with a strictly limited agenda. This would, he urged like his brother Johann, give Franz leisure to read and think [14].

In June 1808 the emperor officially abolished the Konferenzministerium and restored the Staatsrat, using the instructions of 1807 [15]. Only the *Kriegsministerialbüro* (office of the ministry of war) lingered on until 1814, and the only reminder of the great reform was the title of "Staats- und Konferenzminister" that had replaced "Staatsminister". The emperor was sufficiently impressed by Rainer's memorandum to appoint his candidate, Count Karl Zinzendorf as "Dirigierender Staatsminister" and to instruct him to institute weekly conferences and stop all alleinreferieren. He expected a new "spirit" to produce an efficient and forceful government, and ordered the Staatsrat to draw up new appropriate regulations [16].

However, the pressure of the threatening war and then of the war itself, followed by defeat and the disastrous Peace of Schönbrunn that reduced Austria almost to a second-rate power, once again weakened his never

[12] Printed in *OZV*, 163-171.

[13] Walter, *Zentralverwaltung*, 103f.

[14] Wertheimer, *Geschichte*, II, 21-33; Walter, *Zentralverwaltung*, 105-09.

[15] Srbik's statement (*Metternich*, I, 456) that the Staatsrat was "completely abolished" in 1809 is wrong. It functioned from 1808 until 1848. Srbik was probably misled by Metternich's erroneous statement in his Reichsrat plan of 1811 (see chapter IV, below) that the emperor had "abolished the Staatsrat in December 1809". Actually Franz had only announced his intention to give the Staatsrat "a new form" (Krones, *Geschichte*, 73).

[16] Franz's letters printed in *OZV*, 171-74.

overwhelming desire for reform. Instead of strengthening the Staatsrat, Emperor Franz removed important financial matters from its competence. This caused Rainer to complain that there was no point in accepting only some of his proposals. Unless all were implemented, and particularly the most important, "the unification of all branches of the government", the purpose of the reforms would be frustrated [17].

But with the defeat by Napoleon at Wagram, which Emperor Franz blamed on Carl and Johann, the archdukes – excepting the Hungarian Palatine Joseph – had lost all influence. The emperor's new confidant, Zichy, now a minister and much more critical than he had been eighteen months earlier, took up the battle and repeated the old demands for unity of, decisiveness in, and exclusion of trivialities from, the government. His solution was similar to Archduke Rainer's. He proposed to divide the work into three groups – foreign, military and financial affairs – to be dealt with by a weekly ministerial conference; political, economic and judicial matters to be handled in a Staatsrat purged of "the hitherto prevailing spirit of intrigue"; police matters to continue to reach the emperor through his cabinet [18].

Once more Emperor Franz partially accepted and halfheartedly executed the proposals of his adviser. He did not do anything about the ministerial conference since his instructions of June 1808 had essentially covered that though without any visible effect. He reduced the agenda of the Staatsrat in accordance with Zichy's suggestions but the mediocrity – at best – of its members prevented any new spirit from emerging. Nothing really changed [19].

All reform proposals so far had included two principles that the emperor intensely disliked. The first involved some devolution of power to ministers who took a decisive step from advisory to executive status. The second, in one form or another, replaced written procedure by oral deliberation. Hence all proposals, even if accepted, were finally aborted.

With the French alliance affording Austria a period of recuperation, Emperor Franz again turned to a new counsellor. Early in 1811 he asked his Foreign Minister, the only one of the many advisers who had absolutely no connection with, or experience of, internal affairs, for his "views on the reorganization of the Staatsrat". Metternich's ignorance may be ascribed

[17] Walter, *Zentralverwaltung*, 115.

[18] Vortrag Zichy's, October 1809, printed in *OZV*, 174-82.

[19] Hock-Bidermann, *Staatsrat*, 664f.; Walter, *Zentralverwaltung*, 118f. In 1808 Zichy had been promoted from Hofkammerpresident to minister. After Zinzendorf's dismissal in 1809, the Staatsrat contained no minister until 1813.

as much to his foreign origin as to his diplomatic profession. It was, moreover, heightened by the employment of foreign Staatsräte at the Staatskanzlei [20]. Writing to Kübeck in 1842, he admitted his inexperience of the administration as a young minister but pointed out: "I have no knowledge of detail but I do not have to take care of that – let each do his own" [21]. He paid dearly for this ignorance of the administration. Familiarity with its complex structure was to be the chief weapon of his rival Kolowrat in their coming twenty year struggle for power.

[20] Beidtel-Huber, *Staatsverwaltung*, 217ff.

[21] Beer, "Kübeck und Metternich", 29f.

CHAPTER IV

THE REICHSRAT OF 1811

Among the Staatsrat documents in the archives there is an undated report by Metternich from 1811 [1] concerning defects and reform of the "direction of the state machine". It is a good introduction to his approach to reform. The first two paragraphs show that he was already aware of the emperor's idiosyncrasies; they are a masterpiece of ingenuity designed to reassure Emperor Franz that Metternich was not going to waste "precious time" with yet another organizational upheaval "more damaging ... than the defects" themselves. After all, one does not have to destroy the machine in order to repair a small wheel or "pull down a beautiful big house because of – at worst – a rotten doorpost".

Having thus, hopefully, assured a sympathetic hearing, Metternich proceeded – with constant reference to the emperor's "dearest wish", "will" and "sacred promises" – to demand the "completely different organization" of governmental methods he had just disavowed, in order to simplify the business of the "*Centrum*" and rid it of all trivialities. The resultant saving of Emperor Franz's time would benefit the empire by allowing him to learn facts "which never appear in official documents" from newspapers, pamphlets and conversations with "unpretentious local men", celebrated abroad but little known at home [2]. His list of "foremost evils" included verbatim those of Archduke Rainer's memorandum of 1808 plus a few of his own. Like Rainer, too, he objected to alleinreferieren but in much stronger terms and for more detailed reasons. His solution, again quoting the archduke's words verbatim without any acknowledgement, was Rainer's weekly "grosse Konferenz" of Staatsrat members.

[1] "Allgemeine Betrachtungen über die gegenwärtige, und Vorschlag zu einer zweckmässigen Zentralstaatsverwaltung". HHSA, Praes., Kart. 3. Its generalized language and virtual absence of specific proposals indicate that it was written before the Reichsrat plan.

[2] From Franz's point of view this must have been an improvement upon Archdukes Johann's and Rainer's suggestion of reading books and thinking.

He reminded the emperor of the golden age of his early reign and that of his predecessors when a much larger empire easily coped with its business, and pointed out how each successive reform "doubled the work, increased the army of officials" and magnified expenditure. The flood of contradictory and often unworkable instructions, the threat of never imposed penalties, the stress on form to the exclusion of substance – all these brought the government into disrepute at home and abroad, and increased the monarch's work.

The "highest direction" could only be "consolidated" if the emperor put his trust into a "highly respected" Staatsrat "*Kollegium*" (committee) of four ministers and four Staatsräte who were to deal with all important business under Emperor Franz's chairmanship. This would create a "harmony" in all branches of the government without violating secrecy. The four ministers, holding weekly conferences presided over by Franz or a dirigierender Minister, were to call in Staatsräte or Hofstellenpräsidenten where necessary. To unburden the emperor, the Hofstellen must be given greater responsibilities. The suggestion that registrar Grüll, who had already served in Maria Theresia's Staatsrat, be consulted on new instructions for Staatsrat procedure was probably meant to demonstrate the continuity of the institution.

These were Metternich's earliest reflections on internal reform. Mostly unoriginal yet no less radical than his predecessors', he too insisted on the crucial demands for oral deliberation and more confidence in, and power for, ministers. What was new was the psychologically more subtle effort to pay lip-service to the emperor's prejudices and obsessions by playing down the radical nature of the desired changes and presenting them as mere improvements of existing procedures.

Metternich made careful preparations for his report on the reorganization of the Staatsrat. In a letter to Kübeck in 1851 he described how he had studied the concept of the Napoleonic *conseil d'état* as ambassador in Paris, and approvingly quoted the French emperor's words:

> ... il faut un corps composée [sic] d'hommes indépendans [sic], rompus dans les affaires, appelés à rechercher [sic] de la vérité pratique et dont le poids armortira les écarts de L'absolutisme ... .

On the other hand he found Napoleon's "enlightened formula" of government less satisfactory. Bonaparte, "surely one of the most absolutist of spirits", considered his ministers only as proposers of ideas, his *conseil* as examiner of them and himself as final arbiter [3].

[3] *Metternich-Kübeck, Briefwechsel*, 148, 152. On the conseil d'état, see below, p. 129f.

The documents of this period are full of Metternich's notes for the *Reichsrat* (imperial council) plan. They include a detailed study of the French *conseil*, all twenty-five points of which were included verbatim in the report; extracts from Kaunitz's original proposal for the Staatsrat; several drawings of seating plans entitled "*Schemah der Reichsrat Sitzungen*" (model of Reichsrat meetings); a paper contrasting the functions of the Reichsrat and ministerial conferences [4].

This last note is particularly interesting because it shows that Metternich intended from the start to extend his reorganization from the Staatsrat to the entire government, and also because he did not dare to repeat its blunt language in his report. Since it so obviously represents his constitutional ideal – at least under contemporary conditions – it deserves to be fully quoted.

Reichsrat

Everything concerning the legislative power pouvoir legislatif in all branches, justice, finances, military, religious matters, internal administration.

Ministerial Conference

1. Everything concerning the pouvoir executif, hence assuming an already existing law for any order, and where it is only a matter of execution, of eliminating obstacles, clashes, jurisdictional conflicts.
2. Whenever there is something to be changed, improved, added to, regarding the fundamental constitution of the monarchy, of parts thereof.
3. Whenever His Majesty does not wish to decide by himself the question of war or peace, of a treaty to be concluded with a foreign power or to be ratified.
4. Appointments to higher offices, as Prime Ministers, Reichsräte, etc.
5. When any minister desires common consultation with his colleagues; those whose presence is not absolutely necessary may be exempted, but the presiding minister must always be present.

In the report itself [5] neither the power nor the scope of the ministerial conference was spelled out. Metternich merely stressed that it already functioned (he ignored that it practically never met) and suggested it should be continued since it could be useful in "illuminating" a secret subject and in allowing departmental chiefs to confer together. Further subjects for its agenda, he added vaguely, "will no doubt be found".

He then turned to the reform of the Staatsrat. After assuring the emperor that the proposed institution would allow Franz, "the only true central point in the state", to give the government unity and stability, he pointed out where the organization of 1760 had gone wrong. Kaunitz's Staatsrat

[4] All in HHSA, Praes., Kart. 3.

[5] Vortrag Metternich's, April 16, 1811, HHSA, Praes., Kart. 3; almost complete text printed in *OZV*, 182-206; excerpts, differing in some details, in *NP*, II, 444-53.

clashed with the Hofstellen and interfered with their administrative work. The Staatsrat, "*the true council of the sovereign*", as he emphasized, could not be an active or executive body; it aided the monarch as "a giver and custodian of laws". It was the minister, he then asserted boldly, the chief of a department, to whom the monarch had handed part of his executive power. "He must be able to act freely, very freely; in his responsibility lies the guarantee of the state against him". This was the heart of his plan; the rest was mere elaboration, however useful.

At the beginning of his report Metternich gave the emperor three choices as examples for a new Staatsrat constitution: the French conseil d'état, Kaunitz's 1760 Staatsrat, and Russia's of 1810. The essential points of each were outlined but only Napoleon's body was treated at length. The last two were quickly dismissed, the Russian as being too much concerned with judicial and accounting matters, Kaunitz's body because "*without deliberation, without oral debate, no Staatsrat is conceivable*". Here, underlined by Metternich, was the old demand, never before so categorically and incisively formulated.

It was the French conseil, suitably "modified", that served as an example for what Metternich preferred to call Reichsrat instead of Staatsrat in order to stress its validity for the entire monarchy by ending all "distinction between German and Hungarian lands". Its members were to be Staatsminister, Staatsräte and, ex officio, chiefs of the Hofstellen. The monarch was to preside and appoint a minister to take the chair in his absence. The Reichsrat was to be divided into four sections: legislative and judiciary, interior, finance, war. Once or twice a year the emperor was to "assign" all the members to the sections. The agenda and subjects to be debated were to be determined by the emperor [6].

Franz accepted the basic principles of the report and charged Metternich with further elaboration. This is the last we hear of the Reichsrat proposal; nothing further turns up in the documents. Did the emperor realize its implications and drop it? Did Metternich fail to pursue it at his monarch's request? Srbik believes the development of foreign affairs, the slow change from a peace to a war policy, to have preoccupied the emperor [7].

[6] The detailed "Allgemeine Verfassung des Reichsrathes", appended to the report, disagreed with it in several unimportant details.

[7] Srbik, *Metternich*, I, 458. Walter denies this and points out that Franz's letter of February 15, 1814 that started the ball rollling again (see below, chapter V) was sent from the battlefield "amid world-shaking events". (*Zentralverwaltung*, 123). While true, this does not necessarily invalidate Srbik's argument.

Three aspects of the Reichsrat plan are worth closer examination. Where Napoleon's enlightened despotism furnished an example for the regulation of society for the benefit of the state to Emperor Franz, in many ways still the heir of Joseph II [8], Metternich opposed its centralized administration mindful of Joseph's disaster, and advocated the separation of government and administration. The first was to be placed in "the center", the second in the various parts of the empire. This was to become explicit later, particularly in 1817. But already there was more than a hint of it in his criticism of Kaunitz's Staatsrat when he deplored that government (Staatsrat) and administration (Hofstellen) had interfered with each other.

Metternich rejected in the report the concept of a Prime Minister because it could be based "only on the weakness of a monarch and the strength of a minister". That this view derived not merely from a realistic appraisal of Franz's intolerance of any single powerful figure can be seen from a letter written a quarter of a century later. Eighteen months after the emperor's death, when victory over his rival seemed at last to be within his grasp, Metternich wrote to the regent that government by a Prime Minister was the least advisable form because "it can be rooted only in the condition of weakness of a regent and the power of another individual". A Prime Minister would, in short, "be the alter ego of the monarch", a situation leading either to a power struggle or a divided leadership – both undesirable in Metternich's eyes [9].

Krones stressed a personal and political aspect of the Reichsrat plan which, he argued, was partially written in opposition to Baldacci and aimed at his removal from the Staatsrat [10]. As a member of the war party the latter advocated a national war against Napoleon in opposition to Metternich's peace policy [11]. That Baldacci was also an opponent of the Foreign Minister's internal reform was to become obvious in 1814 but was already implicit in 1811. Metternich's plan was close to Archduke Carl's Konferenzministerium in spirit if not in form. Baldacci, an enemy of Carl, had called the latter's reform "extremely defective" in his 1806 memorandum and had

[8] Srbik, "Ideengehalt", 259.

[9] Metternich to Archduke Ludwig, September 30, 1836, printed in Hanns Schlitter, *Aus Oesterreichs Vormärz* (Vienna: Amalthea, 1920), IV, 93-97.

[10] Metternich called the 1807 reorganization of the Staatsrat which had been greatly influenced by Baldacci's 1806 memorandum "the work of a few intriguing subordinate officials".

[11] Krones, *Geschichte*, 192f.

rejected conferences and Staatsrat sessions in favor of the old written procedure [12]. Within three years these two proponents of very opposite reforms were to clash, with Metternich as the apparent winner.

[12] Kübeck, *Tagebücher*, I, 270.

CHAPTER V

THE STAATSRAT OF 1814

On February 15, 1814, from the allied headquarters at Troyes amidst the battles of the Champagne, Emperor Franz sent a letter to Staats- und Konferenzminister Count Josef Wallis [1], informing him that the Staatsrat and the conference, "from now on a connected whole", were to be "the highest central government (*Oberste Zentral-Geschäftsleitung*)". The letter contained details about the intended functions and structures of the two bodies and ordered Wallis to submit as soon as possible a report on how to adapt appropriate new instructions for the Staatsrat to the old ones of 1807. It is not known what caused this sudden resumption of internal reform. It may have been the imminence of victory after two decades of defeat. It is unlikely to have been due to Metternich's influence because, although the latter was present at Troyes and busy with winning the peace against both Napoleon and the Tsar, the content and tenor of the emperor's letter presented a strong contrast to the principles of his Foreign Minister.

Where Metternich had separated Staatsrat and conference, giving one a legislative, the other an executive function, Emperor Franz intended to combine them to create a three tier control with the conference checking the Staatsrat and the latter controlling the Hofstellen. Permanent members of the conference were to take cognizance of the entire work of the Staatsrat, and Franz insisted upon written procedure, "as hitherto" used. Wallis was appointed dirigierender Staatsminister of the Staatsrat, Zichy of the conference. Walter convincingly attributes this clumsy and time-wasting organization to Baldacci with whose 1806 memorandum it had much in common [2]. When Wallis after a delay of two and a half months presented his report implementing Emperor Franz's orders without expressing approval or dissent, it was Baldacci who deplored Wallis' few divergences from the

[1] Printed in *OZV*, 207-11.

[2] Walter, *Zentralverwaltung*, 124-27.

emperor's instructions, thus implying his authorship, and Zichy who protested against Wallis' tactics of delay [3].

In August Metternich entered the fray, having been asked by the emperor to comment on Wallis' work. His report [4] bluntly rejected Emperor Franz's idea of "entangling" Staatsrat and conference because the former would lose its character and the latter would either be crippled or become a "Premierministerium". How can two bodies form a whole, he asked. How can ministries exist if the Staatsrat is entrusted with the central direction? And how can a Staatsrat exist if a conference can revise its decision? "The surest way to paralyze forces is to have them operate against each other". In the proposed organization the Staatsrat would "kill" the ministries and reduce them to "information bureaus". Having pointed out these absurdities, Metternich reiterated his axiom of 1811: the Staatsrat must be the emperor's council of conscience (*Gewissensrat*) dealing only with matters specifically presented to it by the monarch and not concerned automatically with all important business.

Unable to attack Franz, Metternich denounced Wallis, accusing him of ambition to become Prime Minister, of turning the Staatsrat into *his* council by grasping all business and power into his own hand. Despite his "very correct" criticism of Wallis' plan, Baldacci too was condemned for never asking the right questions and for trying to treat symptoms instead of the disease itself. If the emperor really insisted on going through with his ideas, Metternich argued, it would be better to abolish either Staatsrat or conference and to give Wallis his proper title: "First Minister in all internal affairs".

Accompanying this devastating critique were Metternich's own proposals on the organization of ministries, ministerial conference and Staatsrat. Based on his concepts of 1811 with modifications to take account of the "happily changed" political situation (victory and peace), he repeated his demand for a "proper distribution of powers" [5] as the only solution. Having asked for responsible ministers in 1811 [6], he now went one step further

[3] *Ibid.*, 125-27.

[4] Vortrag Metternich's, August 5, 1814, HHSA, Praes., Kart. 3, printed in *OZV*, 212-14, 214-21.

[5] This somewhat grandiloquently named idea had nothing to do with Montesquieu's notions. "The concept of the balance of powers", he wrote, "(posed by Montesquieu) ... is an erroneous idea of the English constitution ... impracticable in its application". (*NP*, VII, 234, 635).

[6] Ministers, that is, who wielded executive power. Metternich distinguished between responsibility "*nach oben*", (i.e. to the monarch), which was natural, and responsibility

to ask for ministries with executive power. Their lack he regarded as a "grave defect" which elsewhere led to "absolute despotism" and in Austria was responsible for the stagnation of the government. There was too much centralization already. The emperor as "the central point" was sufficient; it was now a question of purposefully distributing the business of the government. Finance and war ministries were especially urgent. A ministry of the interior must await "the amalgamation of the various parts of the monarchy" – he was to propose it in 1817. His candidates were Stadion and Fieldmarshal Schwarzenberg as ministers of finance and war. The function of the conference which must never "become an advisory organ" was to enable ministers to consult together and present their collective view to the emperor (who would not be able to ignore it as easily as that of a single minister). Metternich's Staatsrat proposals were virtually identical with those of 1811 except for the abandonment of the name "Reichsrat" which he thought no longer suitable.

Two weeks later Metternich submitted further details of his new Staatsrat plan. There is a curious passage in his covering letter [7] which defends as "compatible" Zichy's double role as president of the ministerial conference as well as of the financial section of the Staatsrat. This contradicts Metternich's insistence on absolute separation of the two bodies. During the 1836 crisis he was to take the opposite position and make Kolowrat's simultaneous membership of the Staatskonferenz and presidency of a Staatsrat section (to say nothing of his domination of the entire Staatsrat) the crucial issue of the dispute. It is likely that in Zichy's case Metternich, who was on excellent terms with him, merely deferred to the wishes of Franz whose favorite Zichy still was. Zichy was, however, at Metternich's suggestion, ordered not to take part in the discussion and vote by his Staatsrat section of matters that were to come before the conference.

In accordance with Metternich's draft, the emperor sent letters to Zichy and Wallis [8] ordering them to draw up, together with the Foreign Minister and the heads of the four sections, new instructions for the Staatsrat on the basis of Metternich's proposals. The latter, encouraged by his success, threw himself into the work of organizing the Staatsrat [9] but it was delayed

"*nach unten*" (i.e. to a parliament, diet, etc.) – a "phantasmagoria" and a "shiboleth" – which was absurd since it would only lead to a paralysis of government, "hence of the public weal". (Vortrag Metternich's, February 9, 1846, fragment, HHSA, Konferenzakten S, No. 61).

[7] Vortrag Metternich's, August 22, 1814, HHSA, Praes., Kart. 3, printed in *OZV*, 221f.

[8] Printed in *OZV*, 222-27.

[9] Metternich to Franz, August 29, 1814, HHSA, Praes., Kart. 3.

by the obstruction of the two military members of the committee who demanded the retention of written procedure and a special status for military affairs. On September 13, again using a draft by Metternich, Emperor Franz appointed the Staatsräte to the four sections. Together with that draft Metternich submitted a proposal [10] to institute equivalent ranks to the *maîtres des réquêtes* and *auditeurs* of the French conseil in order to utilize and train for the Staatsrat talented officials whose low rank did not permit their appointment as Staatsräte. The emperor accepted but the proposal was never implemented.

At the November 6 session of the committee it was decided not to wait any longer to settle the dispute over the organization of the military section but, as the minutes make clear [11], to hand the draft of the new Staatsrat instructions to the emperor for his approval. Franz signed them [12] and ordered them to come into force on December 1. With minor modifications they remained valid until the revolution of 1848.

The two major changes were solely due to Metternich. The Staatsrat was divided into the four sections he had proposed. Each section was to deliberate by itself and report directly to the emperor. Only subjects concerning more than one section were to be dealt with in plenary sessions. The second change prescribed oral discussion for the section meetings. This represented a victory over Wallis who had insisted on changing paragraph 12 of the instructions to retain written opinions to be submitted before the discussion of a subject by those Staatsräte who disagreed with the report by a Referent. Metternich recorded his strong protest in the committee in a dissenting statement [13] in which he charged that the written opinions would once again delay the dispatch of business and impede the free expression of opinion by Staatsräte. Moreover, this mixture of oral and written procedure would produce a hopeless "complication of two opposite methods". Emperor Franz merely noted his agreement in a few lines added to the minutes.

Stadion was put in charge of the finances and of control of the Hofkammer a few weeks after Metternich had proposed his candidature but he was not formally appointed minister of finance until 1816. He worked hard and successfully to revive the shattered finances and the international

[10] Draft and proposal: Vorträge Metternich's, September 12, 1814, HHSA, Praes., Kart. 3; Franz to Wallis, September 13, 1814, printed in *OZV*, 231f.

[11] Protokoll, November 6, 1814, HHSA, Praes., Kart. 3.

[12] "Instruction für den Staatsrat", November 17, 1814, printed in *OZV*, 232-40.

[13] Metternich's votum separatum, November 17, 1814, HHSA, Praes., Kart. 3.

credit of the monarchy after decades of war and loss of territory. When he died in 1824, however, no successor was appointed. The ministry was provisionally directed by the Hofkammerpräsident until Kolowrat persuaded Emperor Franz to abolish it. No minister of war was appointed, nor was a ministry set up. Archduke Carl's surviving Kriegsministerialdepartment, long since without power or influence, was merged with the military section of the Staatsrat. Metternich's regular ministerial conference was similarly stillborn though occasionally conferences did take place; but they remained ineffective and their influence was negligible.

Thus, as usual, reforms accepted in theory were put into effect by half-measures only. But worse was to come. The Staatsrat would not give up its habit of interfering with the Hofstellen, nor the emperor that of calling in experts and others for personal advice. Franz could not overcome his aversion to oral discussion nor get used to presiding over the Staatsrat sessions. He preferred to entrust Wallis with its presidency and to deal instead with the written minutes and resolutions of the Staatsrat and its sections. Gradually the Staatsrat returned to the de facto status of an executive organ, the Kabinettweg was largely restored and the emperor was again overwhelmed with petty work. As the government deteriorated, so criticism mounted and the cycle recommenced [14].

Baldacci used the opportunity of a memorandum on financial and economic matters to inveigh against the Staatsrat's division into sections, against its regular meetings and oral procedure – all ideas borrowed from the "diametrically opposed French council" and quite unsuitable for Austria. He demanded a return to the practice of 1807 (which reflected his own ideas) in order to dispose of business in a "quick, orderly and exact manner" [15]. There were other protests and once more the emperor started his round of consultations and exhortations. Again Metternich produced some useful proposals but they were designed not so much to meet the current dissatisfactions – about which he had said all there was to be said – but to reorganize the entire monarchy on a basis of greater local influence for its various parts.

[14] Srbik, *Metternich*, I, 461; Walter, *Zentralverwaltung*, 134ff.

[15] Franz von Krones, "Freiherr von Baldacci über die inneren Zustände Oesterreichs", *Archiv für oesterreichische Geschichte*, LXXIV (1889), 135-38.

CHAPTER VI

THE NATIONALITIES IN THE REICHSRAT AND CHANCELLERIES

Metternich rejected nationalism – Carlton Hayes' "Jacobin nationalism" – as a "shibboleth" of the revolution, "a phantasmagory of our time", which threatened the dissolution of the "social body", particularly of a multinational empire [1]. Nationalism was, after all, a working form of the doctrine of popular sovereignty. On the other hand he showed respect for, and even interest in, the cultural aspects of "humanitarian nationalism". He pointed out that Austria had never declared Hungarians, Italians or Poles to be Germans, as Napoleon had called "ten to twelve million Germans and Italians" French. His aim was the "living together of the various peoples in a mutually beneficial association" [2].

Although he regarded the German nationality to be "preeminent" in Austria, as being that of the reigning dynasty and as the "civilizing element" of the monarchy [3], he strongly opposed Joseph's II policy of centralization, as well as his practice of germanization, condemning centralization as "the most absurd of all the tyrannies" [4]. Since he saw Austria as a "federal state" or even as a "confederacy (*Staatenverband*)" [5], he wanted to strike a balance between "union and separation" [6]. He found his own solution for the perennial Habsburg problem of creating "unity combined with diversity" in the concept that unity of government did not exclude diversity

[1] *NP*, VII, 205, 317, 357.

[2] *NP*, VII, 207.

[3] *NP*, VII, 388.

[4] *NP*, I, 269-71; VII, 209, 612.

[5] *NP*, III, 66; VIII, 512. Metternich's concept of a federal Austria seems to have evolved slowly. In 1817 he qualified "federal state" by "as little as this expression can be taken here in the usual sense, I cannot find a better one to replace it". In 1851 he declared flatly: "The great complex of lands making up the Austrian empire is a confederacy and the empire is thus unlike any other".

[6] *NP*, VIII, 429f.; *Metternich-Kübeck Briefwechsel*, 105.

in administration, with the latter adapting to and respecting the geographical, historical and cultural differences of the provinces [7].

He was not alone in holding this opinion. In 1815 the "*Einrichtungskommission*" (commission for organization) set up to inquire into the, reintroduction of the former estate constitutions of Tirol and Vorarlberg, returned to Austria by the Congress of Vienna, introduced its affirmative report with a similar reflection:

> The Austrian monarchy must abandon the idea of total uniformity in the administration. The subjects of this vast empire are not *one* nation, *one* people ... [8].

Acting on this assumption, Metternich had already in 1815 proposed that the emperor be crowned [9] in the presence of deputies from the estates of all provinces. This act of common homage, he had hoped, would symbolize the unity of the empire while the estates were to be assured of keeping or regaining their constitutions [10]. By 1816, with peace restored, the time seemed ripe for a further installment of internal reform including the transfer from temporary administration to permanent status of the recently returned and newly acquired Italian and Illyrian provinces. Hence Metternich offered what he was to call "the only practical solution of the great task of rendering feasible the political coexistence (*staatliche Zusammenleben*) of the various peoples of the empire by means of an organic association" [11].

His Reichsrat [12] proposal, apparently written late in 1816 and presented to Franz early next year, has been lost. Despite strenuous efforts by Metter-

[7] *NP*, VII, 248; VIII, 396f., 422, 474, 520-23. For Metternich's policy regarding the restored and newly acquired territories, see Arthur G. Haas, *Metternich, Reorganization and Nationality 1813-1818* (Wiesbaden: Steiner, 1963).

[8] Hermann Meynert, *Kaiser Franz I: Zur Geschichte seiner Regierung und seiner Zeit* (Vienna: Hölder, 1872), 239.

[9] Franz had never been crowned with the new crown of "Austria", created in 1804.

[10] *NP*, I, 218. Metternich distinguished between "estate constitutions (*Landesständische Verfassungen*)", of which he approved, and "a so-called representative system" which he considered fatal, as he carefully explained to Friedrich Wilhelm III of Prussia and to his Staatsminister (*NP*, III, 174f., 265). He also approved of "constitution" by which he meant governmental framework or structure. Thus: "No state can exist *without a constitution*, while none can thrive under the demands of *constitutionalism*". (*Metternich-Hartig Briefwechsel*, 83). In this connection it should perhaps be stressed that his concept of a federal Austria excluded any "representative" character of its structure, either in the center or in the provinces. He regarded "superimposed parliaments" (on federal and provincial level) an "impossibility" and "absurd". (*NP*, VIII, 471, 478).

[11] Alexander von Hübner, *Ein Jahr meines Lebens* (Leipzig: Brockhaus, 1891), 12.

[12] In the 1811 plan the term "Reichsrat" was synonymous with "Staatsrat". The Reichsrat proposed in 1816-17 was probably meant to function alongside the Staatsrat.

nich himself in the forties, by the editors of his *Nachgelassene Papiere*, and by many historians to locate it in the archives, no trace has ever been found [13]. It is known only through scattered comments among Metternich's letters and papers. Writing to Prince Felix Schwarzenberg in 1849, he advocated his "Vormärz idea" of a "meeting of deputies from provincial estates to form a joint representation in the seat of the government" [14]. In an undated note, probably meant for his autobiography and written after 1848, he declared his purpose to be "the strengthening of the empire" through "legislative adjustment of the parts and the uniform reinforcement of the central power in the legislative and administrative fields". To achieve this, the note adds the following tantalizing details:

Estate representation existed in the [provinces], they had therefore to be created in the center. ... Hence I proposed besides a revision of the estates situation the creation of a Reichsrat that was to consist of deputies from the estates and of members appointed by the emperor. The jurisdiction of this newly to be created central point was to be the examination of the budget and of those laws which concerned the generality [15].

Thus it is clear, even with all details lost, that the plan involved a rather tame Reichsrat with limited scope. Its membership, representing not the "peoples" but the narrowly based provincial estates, was to be diluted by Reichsräte nominated by the emperor. Judging by the "central representation" of estates that Metternich recommended to Prussia in 1818, he probably believed the Reichsrat would be similarly "easy to guide towards the good" because it would be composed of "individual, mutually hostile deputies – far from ready to unite for *one* purpose of state" [16].

Metternich repeated the story of the fate of his plan many times. He described to Hartig how Emperor Franz put the proposal into his drawer "in which much good as well as much bad remained buried". Ten years later, having recovered from a serious illness, the emperor apologized to Metternich for having neglected his plan. Metternich stressed the urgency to "erect a governmental machine which would aid his successor". After another eight years Franz again regretted to have done nothing and promised to act very soon this time; within two months he died without having been

[13] *NP*, II, 74f.; Alfred Stern, "L'idée d'une representation centrale de l'Autriche conçu par le Prince de Metternich", *Revue Historique*, XXXI (1886), 313-26.

[14] *NP*, VIII, 478.

[15] *NP*, III, 74f.

[16] *NP*, III, 175.

able to do so [17]. The emperor's reluctance to create the Reichsrat was probably due as much to his opposition to accord any meaningful role to the estates as to the radical departure from traditional form involved in the scheme.

According to the editors of his papers, Metternich "cooperated" in the restoration of the estate constitutions to the regained provinces. They refer to his "encouraging influence" without being able to document it [18]. The estates, the embodiment of conservative territorial particularism, represented the social, and to some extent political, interests of the nobility, gentry, clergy and the small upper stratum of the bourgeoisie. Since Maria Theresia's reforms they had been reduced to minor roles in local welfare and taxation matters, and to the empty ceremonial of the *Landtage* which maintained in antiquarian form the status of the ancient crownlands under the powerful reality of the centralized state. Joseph II ruthlessly abolished their constitutions when they seemed to stand in the way of his reforms. After his death partial restoration included the rights to petition and to grant taxes; the right to be consulted in new legislation was added by Leopold II [19].

Emperor Franz followed his father reluctantly in the restoration of estate privileges, admonishing the Landtage to set an example to "the other classes" of obeying the laws instead of claiming special exemptions from them. He regarded, as he wrote to Metternich, "the participation of estates in legislative matters doubtful". Alarmed by the power of the Hungarian diet which represented much more than mere medieval tradition, he insisted that estate constitutions be granted only by grace of the emperor and not by ancient right. It took the estates of Vorarlberg eighteen years of reports and deliberations to achieve their purely advisory powers [20].

Gradually all estate rights fell into disuse. Estate officials were increasingly employed by the imperial provincial administration. Since their most important section, the nobility, found employment in the bureaucracy

[17] *Metternich-Hartig Briefwechsel*, 42-44. Other versions, with slight variations of details and dates: *Metternich-Kübeck Briefwechsel*, 149f.; Hübner, *Ein Jahr*, 11f.; *NP*, III, 75; VII, 612f.; VIII, 509ff.

[18] *NP*, III, 98.

[19] Robert A. Kann, *Das Nationalitätenproblem der Habsburgermonarchie* (2nd ed. Graz-Cologne: Böhlaus Nf., 1964), I, 64ff.; Redlich, *Reichsproblem*, I/1, 39; I/2, 9ff.; On the role of the estates in the first half of the nineteenth century, see Springer, *Geschichte*, I, 509-49; Bibl, *Niederoesterreichische Stände im Vormärz*.

[20] Meynert, *Kaiser Franz*, 229; *NP*, III, 269; Friedrich Engel-Janosi, "Zur Genesis der Revolution von 1848", *Zeitschrift für öffentliches Recht*, III (1922/23), 574-80.

and prestige in their support of the throne, the estates acquiesced in the loss of their rights, rejoiced in the brilliant red and silver uniforms provided by Emperor Franz, and contented themselves with granting whatever taxes the emperor demanded and with collecting them for him [21].

Only with the slowly increasing pauperization of the nobility [22], with the growing restlessness of all classes, and with the mounting frustration of the more intelligent officials in the early forties, did an estate-led opposition movement gain significance, particularly in Bohemia and Lower Austria [23]. It might have seemed logical to a conservative at this time to turn to the ancient Estates of the Realm as a foundation for governmental reform. But Metternich rejected that. He would not go much further than Franz had gone in granting concessions to them. "Let them consent", he wrote to Kolowrat in 1846, "but not take the initiative" [24].

Having failed with his Reichsrat plan, Metternich returned a few months later to his favorite subject of separating government from administration and to his demand for ministers with executive powers. With his new proposal he sent a covering letter to Emperor Franz intended to put him into a receptive mood [25]. His plan, he promised, would be presented in "simple sentences"; having been "considered and examined" over "a long period of probation", his proposal contained "nothing shrill, no revolutionary change, not a single daring principle". Indeed, "it does not even need a reform aiming to upset the regular forms, but only an organization of the parts – the already existing organic parts – of the central government". He now added a warning to provide for the future, in terms recalling those of Archduke Carl ten years earlier. Let the emperor as a father consider how, "in its present manner", the government would function without him. "A weak successor" would be unable to execute the necessary change to provide a strong organization for the "first main springs of the government". This change could not be left to the emperor's "last period of life" because it took years for both "director" and "tools" to get used to their "new sphere of action".

[21] Bibl. *Niederoesterreichische Stände im Vormärz*, 30-38; Beidtel-Huber, *Staatsverwaltung*, 49.

[22] Bibl, *Niederoesterreichische Stände im Vormärz*, 53-56; Springer, *Geschichte*, I, 165.

[23] Already in 1836 one of the highest officials warned that the Bohemian estates might make trouble for the government and become "an instrument for bad tendencies" unless they were disciplined. (Clam-Martinitz to Metternich, August 8, 1836, HHSA, Staatskanzlei, Korrespondenz, Fasz. 91 [hereafter cited as "Staatskanzlei, K."]).

[24] HHSA, Minister Kolowrat Akten, 748 ex 1846.

[25] *NP*, III, 62-66.

The introduction of the proposal itself [26] reverts to the federal character of Austria and the unique position of its monarch who wore the crowns of the various parts as well as that of Austria. A geopolitical reflection on its strategic position concludes that "Austria needed a greater effort at self-preservation" than any other great power except Prussia. The "true and free power required" could only result from "clearly and firmly expressed and applied principles". A repetition of the Josephinian policy of "total fusion of all parts of the monarchy" would not only be bound to fail but would involve "today" the "idea of a central representation". Having frightened Franz, Metternich hastened to reassure him that the alternative policy, the "preservation" of the special and traditional cultural and historical varieties of the provinces under a strong and well organized central government, would involve only "the slightest modification of already existing governmental norms". In fact, "the defect could be remedied" with "one word by the monarch, with a single measure". This defect was the extreme variation in the policy of the empire towards its nations. While Hungary and Transylvania enjoyed privileges to the point of independence, other provinces suffered from the tendencies towards fusion and centralization that "degenerated into a mania to interfere in details" which "was fatal to the spirit of government".

Metternich divided the government into seven branches: external affairs, internal affairs, finances, war, justice, police, and accounting. Each of these branches was functionally separated into a policy-making ("moral", as he called it) part and an administrative ("manipulative" or "technical") part. He expressed the core of his proposal in simplest terms, as promised: the two parts must of necessity be separate; the administrative part which executed the policy of the governmental part must be subordinated to the latter. In words reminiscent of Archduke Carl's 1802 memorandum, Metternich defined the difference between the function and designation of minister and Hofstellenpräsident. The latter, also having executive power, "is only the head of a deliberative board" whose character destroyed "the so necessary individual responsibility". The minister is charged with that responsibility but might retain as much of the board procedure as he might find useful in his own department [27].

[26] Metternich's memorandum, October 27, 1817, HHSA, Kaiser Franz Akten, Fasz. 82, printed in *OZV*, 325-33. *NP*, III, 66-73 is incomplete.

[27] This definition of the president-minister distinction was added in a marginal note in Metternich's own hand; it is omitted in *NP*, III, 71. For more details of his ambiguity towards the board system, see above, p. 6.

This separation of powers had already been carried out successfully in the ministry of finance; it was now time to set up ministries of justice and interior. Police and accounting, on the other hand, were not really suitable as ministries (perhaps Metternich did not want to propose too many changes at once). It was to the ministry of the interior that he devoted the rest of his memorandum. Its head was to bear the title Supreme Chancellor and Minister of the Interior. Directly under him, forming the ministry together with him, were to be four national chancellors, each responsible for a region consisting of several provinces: a Bohemian-Moravian-Galician chancellor; an Austrian one for the German speaking alpine provinces; an Illyrian one for Carinthia, Carniola, Istria and part of Croatia and Dalmatia; an Italian one for Lombardy and Venetia.

Within the ministry he envisaged a sort of balance of power between unity and diversity: the minister was to be "the guardian and representative of governmental unity", defending the principle of unity "in the most enlightened spirit possible in the given situation". The four chancellors were to represent and advocate "against him" the local interests of their regions. Oral discussion was to be the ministry's procedure. The relation of the existing Hungarian and Transylvanian chancelleries with the new ones were left open except for a vague statement that the new arrangements would bring them down from "their present high level", as a first step towards eventual reorganization.

This was Metternich's third proposal on internal reform, his most ambitious and significant one, logically based upon his previous two. What was the emperor going to do about it? After a few weeks' reflection he asked the governor of Lombardy and former minister of finance Count Franz Saurau for his opinion of the memorandum. Hardly mentioning any part of Metternich's proposal in his report [28], Saurau congratulated Emperor Franz on the "simplification and concentration of administrative matters" which would bestow "new and immeasurable benefits" on the greater part of the empire. This non-commital attitude hardly augured well for the spirit of Metternich's work when Saurau was appointed Supreme Chancellor and Minister of the Interior within a week. But in Franz's letter of guidance, accompanying the appointment, and in the official announcement of the creation of the new ministry [29] Metternich's scheme was already watered

[28] Saurau's report, December 18, 1817, HHSA, Kaiser Franz Akten, Fasz. 82, excerpts printed in Schlitter, *Vormärz*, IV, 91.

[29] Franz to Saurau, December 23, 1817, printed in *OZV*, 333-35; announcement in *Wiener Zeitung*, December 24, 1817, printed in Haas, *Metternich and Reorganization*, 180f. *NP*, III, 73 is wrong in several details.

down to the point of wrecking it. The emperor upset the plan's balance by stressing unity of the empire and "uniform principles" at the expense of provincial "peculiarities". He further weakened Metternich's concept of national balance and respect for national differences by creating only three chancellors, combining "Austria" with Illyria[30]. Actually Franz did not even appoint an Austro-Illyrian chancellor but only a "substitute" vice-chancellor. Finally the rejection of a ministry of justice was indicated by the appointment of Wallis as president of the existing Oberste Justizstelle. This made an effective ministerial conference as far away as ever.

Saurau has been described as "enlightened" [31]; Kübeck found him "witty and reasonable" but "superficial" and disputed his reputation as a liberal, declaring him to be "as liberal as Cardinal Richelieu might have been" [32]. Perhaps this reputation derived from his anti-clericalism; Saurau was a Josephinian bureaucrat (he had been governor [*Stadthauptmann*] of Vienna under Joseph II) who offered quiet but effective opposition to Emperor Franz's procrastination and hostility to reform, as well as to Metternich's influence on internal affairs [33]. Under his direction the ministry of the interior never exceeded the scope of a Hofstelle and soon developed centralizing tendencies. His successors, after 1830, were mediocre and incompetent; they lost, significantly, the title of Minister of the Interior, being appointed Supreme Chancellors only [34].

Metternich's third proposal thus fared no better than the previous two. Henceforth, until Emperor Franz's death, he confined himself with only minor exceptions to recalling his earlier plans and to demanding the proper execution of those parts that the emperor had accepted. Where, in short, the letter had been conceded, he vainly sought to provide the spirit.

[30] Metternich himself had already reduced the number of chancellors from a possible seven to six. As his friend, Prince Franz Dietrichstein, with whom he discussed his plan, pointed out to him, the combination of Galicia and Bohemia-Moravia would create a "ridicously large" region. He did not point out that the Czechs and Poles had very little in common. (Hass, *Metternich and Reorganization*, 121f., 177).

[31] By the diplomat Johann von Wessenberg, Foreign Minister in 1849 (Corti, *Metternich*, II, 372).

[32] Kübeck, *Tagebücher*, I, 439.

[33] Srbik, *Metternich*, I, 453.

[34] *Ibid.*, 463; Walter, *Zentralverwaltung*, 247. For comments on Saurau's successors, see Kübeck, *Tagebücher*, I, 357, 456, 663, 806f.

CHAPTER VII

MOUNTAINS IN LABOR

After Metternich's digression into the field of decentralization and a more equitable balance of national interests during 1817, attention focussed again on the old twin evils of overburdening of government and monarch with trivial administrative decisions, and of the false position and function of the Staatsrat. The emperor urged the Hofstellen in vain to "make immediate decisions instead of writing reports". Franz could not rouse them from their "timidity and indolence", or prevent them from producing memoranda "at the least hint of doubt and hesitation". Nor could the mistrustful emperor himself refrain from breaking his own rules in order to ensure that his wishes had been complied with in some insignificant matter [1].

With the situation thus as unsatisfactory as ever, Emperor Franz indulged in his favorite substitute for action. He started another round of asking for reports on how to reorganize the government, for opinions of reports, and for critiques of opinions of reports. The first to be consulted was Zichy. His report of 1821 [2] analyzed the practical results of the instructions issued to the Staatsrat in 1814 in a kind of balance sheet. The advantage of the new organization had evidently satisfied Metternich's expectations. The division into sections and the oral procedure had accelerated the governmental process and had allowed free expression of varied opinions by Staatsräte and a better formulation of resolutions.

On the other hand, there were drawbacks to be recorded too. Delay was caused by keeping the majority of documents for the next session, sometimes for weeks, instead of coming to a quick decision. The lack of cooperation between sections in matters that concerned more than one of them not

[1] Quoted in Walter, *Zentralverwaltung*, 136.

[2] Vortrag Zichy's, undated (probably November or December 1821), HHSA, Kaiser Franz Akten, Kart. 43, Fasz. 41.

only contributed to delay but also to ignorance by one section of the opinions of others. The sectional division, Zichy concluded, had also undermined the Staatsrat's central direction and "unity of principles" because there was little connection and communication among heads of sections.

His solutions included a shortened procedure to reduce delays and lighten the emperor's work load; a suggestion to bring the military section into closer contact with the other three; the combination of the judicial, internal and financial sections – or at least of the last two – under one chief. An opportunity for the last proposal was at hand since neither the judicial nor the internal section had a permanent head at the moment.

The emperor accepted the new instructions Zichy had appended to his report and ordered him to submit suggestions for a reduction of the Staatsrat agenda. But before Zichy's report had reached Emperor Franz it was given to two other ministers for their comments. It is not clear whether Zichy handed it to Metternich on his own initiative (they were on very good terms) or at the emperor's bidding. Metternich himself showed it to Stadion and asked for his criticism.

The Minister of Finance had three important points to make. He agreed with Metternich that the Staatsrat was the emperor's own council, his "Gewissensrat", and that its agenda was therefore to be determined by the monarch alone. From this he drew two logical conclusions which went to the heart of the governmental malady. On the one hand, "the emperor must not ... make administrative decisions that had not been discussed in the Staatsrat". On the other, "the Hofstellen must be given detailed instructions on what subjects *alone* they had to report to His Majesty". But that meant also that the emperor must be "persuaded not to demand from the Hofstellen thousands of reports that were quite outside this designated limit. At least five sixths of the reports now submitted to the emperor would then be eliminated". Finally, Stadion agreed with Zichy, while preferring a separate chief for each section, that the Staatsrat as a whole needed a head – a president or one of the section chiefs – to preside over sessions and to supervise all procedures [3].

This was the point at which Metternich joined issue with his colleagues. In his own report [4] he stressed that the sectional division was "one of the foundations of the new regulation" whose advantages Zichy had fully

[3] Walter, *Zentralverwaltung*, 138f.

[4] Vortrag Metternich's, December 6, 1821, HHSA, Praes., Kart. 4. Another version, dated December 16, is in the HHSA, Kaiser Franz Akten, Kart. 43. It repeats exactly the same content in more elegant language; the only exception will be noted below.

demonstrated. The same motives applied to "the presiding individuals too". He therefore opposed the grouping of several sections under one chief. The most he would concede was a temporary joining of the financial and interior sections in cases in which "one individual ... with equal experience of both sections" could take charge of both, but that could never be a permanent arrangement and would merely prove that only one competent man could be found where two were needed. The judicial section, Metternich emphasized, had "at all times" to be under a separate head.

On the question of personnel he declared flatly that the Staatsrat, with few exceptions, was "really desolate". It was a matter of "urgency to revive it through the appointment of new individuals". One of the exceptions was apparently Zichy for whose knowledge, talents and attitude Metternich had high praise and whose ability he wanted harnessed to the task of reconstructing the Staatsrat procedure. Hence he recommended that Zichy be entrusted temporarily with the direction of the internal section in addition to his financial one.

Metternich expressed satisfaction with Zichy's analysis and proposals, and added his own comments on the inadequacies of the current Staatsrat which he attributed to two defects. The first was the already mentioned low calibre of its personnel, the second the misunderstanding of the principles of its purpose and scope. He stressed again the concept of a Gewissensrat without executive power, designed to advise the monarch on those problems he specifically submitted to it. Unless the Staatsrat confined itself to such important questions as new legislation or deciding between conflicting opinions by the administration, "it descends from the sphere of higher supervision to the lower field of activity".

He also reiterated his old demand: "In our general governmental structure the highest link in the ascending chain, *an appropriate ministerial conference* is lacking". This sentence is omitted in the December 16 version of the report. Perhaps Metternich decided that asking the emperor to change the function of the Staatsrat was a sufficiently irritating demand; to ask for more might risk another recourse by Franz to his notorious drawer.

Having obtained the opinions of his senior ministers, Emperor Franz did nothing for several months. In the summer of 1822 he finally decided that he needed more advice and handed Zichy's and Metternich's reports to Kübeck whom, as a sign of his confidence, he had recently appointed Staats- und Konferenzrat [5]. Kübeck's critique [6] first summarized the other

[5] Kübeck, *Tagebücher*, I, 286.

[6] Vorträg Kübeck's, July 15, 1822, HHSA, Kaiser Franz Akten, Kart. 43.

reports and strongly supported Metternich's interpretation that the Staatsrat was not an executive organ and hence had "no influence on the agenda assigned to it". He also agreed that its function was to provide a "thorough, ... comprehensive ... impartial" opinion "in due time" on whatever question the emperor submitted to it. Three methods, in basic agreement with Zichy, seemed essential to Kübeck to accomplish this purpose. First, the Staatsrat must be divided not only into sections but also into subsections, "*Referate*", consisting of individual subjects handled by specialists. Secondly, in order to treat all problems speedily and comprehensively, there must be oral discussion of specialists' written reports. Thirdly – and here he disagreed with Metternich – he quoted the Staatsrat instructions declaring it to "form one body" and concluded that it therefore needed one director to supervise its personnel, its work, particularly where it concerned more than one section, and the distribution of its agenda.

All three ministers and Kübeck thus agreed that the Staatsrat should only be an advisory body with a special agenda. They were satisfied that the sectional division and oral procedure had demonstrated their merits but could still be improved. Three of them convincingly argued for a unified direction of the entire Staatsrat. Metternich's rather weak objections to this raise the suspicion that he might have been afraid of the potentiality of an influential rival. The next two and a half decades were to prove that this fear was well founded. Stadion alone had the courage – and, apart from Metternich, the prestige – to admonish the emperor to observe his own rules, though he doubted that Franz would ever "consent" to abandon his arbitrary "*Kabinettspraxis*" (the habit of private consultations). Nevertheless, he encouraged Metternich – in vain – to do something about it [7].

As a result of all these reports Emperor Franz issued, a year later, a very short supplement of four points to the 1814 Staatsrat instructions, using verbatim that part of the summary in Kübeck's report that had dealt with speeding up the procedure in cases of unanimous agreement of the Staatsräte. It was indeed, as Walter justly commented, a case of "pariunt montes, nascitur mus!" [8].

[7] Already as Foreign Minister, in a note to the ministry of war in 1807, Stadion had accused Franz of being responsible "for every defect of the administration", because his "direct interference in detail" had the effect of depriving "high and low servants of the monarchy" of responsibility and will power. (Walter, *Zentralverwaltung*, 240f.).

[8] Franz to Zichy, August 12, 1823, HHSA, Praes., Kart. 4, printed in *OZV*, 240f. Walter's comment in *Zentralverwaltung*, 144.

Not surprisingly this was the last big debate on reform of the Staatsrat during Franz's reign. Metternich offered only one more proposal [9], in 1825, which he probably thought would have a chance of success because it was of relatively minor importance and of major assistance to the emperor himself. Following once more the "ideal" example of the French conseil d'état, the civil administration, he suggested, needed a kind of administrative tribunal analogous to an appeals court in juridical matters. It would deal with private claims of individuals who believed themselves injured by actions of governmental institutions, "even the highest in the state". This tribunal, in the shape of a committee headed by Archduke Ludwig, was to form a fifth section of the Staatsrat. Its function was to sift all claims and complaints, to act upon most of them by itself, and to submit to the monarch only the most important ones. The new committee was to "remain a state secret", presumably to make it easier for Franz to initiate a change if all decisions were to remain in his name at least. Metternich's civil rights proposal bears no acknowledgment by the emperor; it seems to have disappeared in his drawer.

This was Metternich's last attempt to initiate any reform of the government. For the next decade he was reduced to defending the existing organization, so inadequate in his eyes, from attacks which tried to turn it into a power base for rival ambitions.

[9] Vortrag Metternich's, March 1, 1825, HHSA, Praes., Kart. 4.

CHAPTER VIII

TRIUMPH AND FRUSTRATION

The paternal bureaucratic absolutism which his enemies named after Metternich and which Hartig preferred to call "Franz's system", has also been called the "Colloredo system" [1], after the emperor's tutor, confidant, chief chamberlain, first and only Kabinettminister, and originator of the notorious "Kabinettweg" mentioned earlier. Whatever the name, by 1809, when Metternich was appointed foreign minister, the system was already in full flower. "It is by no means new", as Count Josef Sedlnitzky, the president of the Polizeihofstelle, explained in 1821, "His Majesty has had it always. Only now he was lucky enough to have found the organs which truly reflect it" [2]. Metternich, one of the organs, accepted the basis of the system which Hartig defined as "absolute maintenance of the sovereign's rights and denial of any claims by the people to share these rights" [3].

From the beginning, however, conscious of the shortcomings and weaknesses of the system, Metternich sought to improve its organization and operation. As we have seen, soon after coming to power in 1809 he made a determined effort to introduce important reforms based on the experience of his predecessors and his own observation. He had the confidence of a man in his prime – he was thirty-eight in 1811 – who was the first to enjoy the emperor's full trust since the departure of Franz Colloredo in 1805.

Metterich's first fifteen years in office saw his greatest triumps in foreign policy. Thanks partly to his brilliant diplomacy, Austria rose from defeat to become one of the arbiters of Europe with Metternich virtually assuming the leadership of the continent. These same years also saw the series of well argued, practical proposals to reform the clumsy and backward Austrian government in order to create a strong state – strong finan-

[1] Beidtel-Huber, *Staatsverwaltung*, 20-26.

[2] Quoted in Bibl, *Zerfall*, I, 44.

[3] Hartig, *Genesis*, 38.

cially, administratively and militarily – capable of playing the ambitious role he had assigned to it in the European constellation. In this "moral pentarchy" [4] which governed Europe, each great power was to combat, at home and abroad, what Gentz called the "burning fever" of "a new social order" [5].

The Foreign Minister divided his time and energy between the demands of foreign and internal affairs: peace with Napoleon – the 1811 Reichsrat plan – maneuvering between Napoleon and the Tsar – the 1814 Staatsrat proposals – reordering Europe – reordering the monarchy (Reichsrat and ministry of the interior) – controlling Europe through congresses – Staatsrat reform. It was an alternation between triumph and frustration.

Metterlich diagnosed the malady of the government in a letter written two weeks before the revolution of 1848 to Count Ludwig Ficquelmont who a fortnight later was to succeed him as Foreign Minister.

> Bureaucracy does not move; it is static by nature. Its lower strata, instead of carrying the higher ones, lean upon them. Administration takes the place of government, and the government disappears under the weight of details that crush it. ... In the end this moral and material nonsense drowns the head of the state in a flood of detailed questions and deprives the state itself of all action [6].

In a letter to the emperor concerned with Count Franz Kolowrat's resignation in 1830, and in a draft for this letter [7], Metternich used the occasion to introduce a summary of his internal policy by pointing to "three chief principles" or "necessities unfulfilled by us":

1) The correct designation of the activity of highest administrative authorities.
2) Their cooperation in a ministerial conference.
3) A proper separation of the activity of the *administrating* Hofstellen and of the *controlling* Staatsrat.

These three points contain his basic ideas of governmental structure and function which he maintained, essentially unchanged, throughout his life.

The separation of policy making and administration was a subject whose importance he already hinted at in 1811, made a cardinal point of in 1814 and presented as almost the first demand in the memorandum of advice he sent to Pope Pius IX on the government of the papal states in 1846 [8].

[4] *NP*, I, 219.
[5] *NP*, III, 168.
[6] *NP*, VII, 572.
[7] Draft undated; Metternich to Franz, January 19, 1830, both in HHSA, Staatskanzlei, P.M. The draft, significantly, deals only with reform, the letter with Kolowrat as well.
[8] *NP*, VII, 246-52.

He still preached it years after the revolution of 1848. A separation served a twofold purpose. First, it relieved the government from trivialities which only caused delay and confusion. Secondly, such a separation strengthened the government at the center while respecting the historical and cultural individuality of the provinces by "reserving" administration for "the parts". Metternich recognized the polyglot character of the monarchy and tried to find a proper if limited place for diversity in his reform proposals of 1817. The emperor rejected this farsighted attempt to deal realistically with this problem because recognition of it would in his opinion derogate from his absolute rule.

In the government itself Metternich demanded a "distribution of powers". He largely ignored the judicial aspect but was very explicit on the executive and legislative (or advisory) branches. He explained his idea of the latter to Kübeck in 1851:

> I have always recognized as an important element of the mechanism called government the existence of an advisory institution without executive power. The name – Staatsrat or Reichsrat etc. – is irrelevant; it must be a morally independent, well organized body consisting of qualified personalities. It will then provide reassurance to ministers and give confidence to the public [9].

He varied somewhat in outlining the functions of this council. In 1836 he defined the Staatsrat as "guardian of the norm" and regarded it as charged with ensuring "that the several parts of the empire do not have their special rights injured". The Staatsrat "is placed *behind* the throne", was his way of emphasizing that it was the emperor's privy council charged solely with advising him as the "guide of the conscience of the sovereign", as he described it to Pius IX [10] – it was not an independent institution [11].

From the beginning, however, it was the ministerial conference that he considered most important and advocated most urgently. Summing up his policy to Ficquelmont one week after his resignation in 1848, he enumerated all his proposals (Reichsrat, strong Staatsrat, ministries, etc.) and it was only the ministerial council that he underlined [12]. From the very first he stressed the importance of providing ministers with responsibility for departments and with executive power. To the degree that he promoted

[9] *Metternich-Kübeck Briefwechsel*, 151.

[10] Metternich to Ficquelmont, December 14, 1836, printed in Eduard von Wertheimer, "Fürst Metternich und die Staatskonferenz", *Oesterreichische Rundschau*, X (1907), 54.

[11] *NP*, VII, 248f.

[12] *NP*, VII, 613.

the power of a conference of ministers, he confined the Hofstellen to purely administrative matters and reduced the importance of the Staatsrat by demoting it from its *de facto* status of a *Zentralbehörde* (central authority) to that of an advisory council. This sponsorship of the conference, in one form or another, became much more pronounced after 1828 when his rival increasingly dominated the Staatsrat for his own purposes. Kübeck noted in his diary that Metternich never liked the Staatsrat; it was an "object of jealousy and hate" because of its independence from him and because it weakened his influence upon the emperor [13].

There was a procedural point too, that he persistently defended against the opposition of Franz and after the emperor's death, of Archduke Ludwig. Both loathed conferences and oral discussions. They preferred the cumbersome and chaotic method of circulating written reports, written "votes" on the reports, and "recirculation" and "revoting" of all written opinions, piling memoranda on memoranda. This seemed to Metternich a disastrous waste of time and an obstacle to a clear and unprejudiced expression of opinions which destroyed the effectiveness of central authority. Instead of formulating precise questions and furthering clear cut decisions, this routine bogged down the government in a hopeless morass of paper work. From the perspective of the twentieth century the amount of time expended on penmanship alone is staggering. "Governing", as he wrote in 1837, "means coordinating, ... this can only be reached through the method of discussion" [14]. It was accordingly one of his prime objectives to introduce the fresh air of discussion into the airless chamber of the imperial scribe.

Among all those who had proposed reforms – Archdukes Carl and Rainer, Saurau, Stadion and Zichy – Metternich alone possessed the ability to present his proposals logically, with incisive argument, compelling serious consideration of them in the "all-highest" place. Owing to the prestige of his foreign policy, he succeeded in leaving a more lasting mark on the Austrian government than any of his predecessors since the retirement of Prince Kaunitz.

Not that the emperor willingly acepted his proposals. He accepted them reluctantly and put them into effect only half-heartedly with half-measures [15]. In his incurable aversion to change, he was soon ready to listen

[13] Kübeck, *Tagebücher*, I, 381.

[14] *NP*, VI, 211.

[15] "Auf halben Wegen und zu halber Tat mit halben Mitteln zauderhaft zu streben" as Grillparzer has an earlier Habsburg emperor describe "the curse of our noble house" in *Ein Bruderzwist in Habsburg*, II, 2, written in 1848.

sympathetically to trifling objections by petty minded officials and members of his entourage. Such men worked ceaselessly to sabotage nearly all of the new rules and practices inspired by Metternich until they were gradually neglected and finally completely ignored.

The opposition to Metternich's internal reforms, encouraged by the monarch, came from numerous members of the highest Austrian nobility – many of whom were jealous of Metternich as a foreigner – and of the upper strata of the deracinated Josephinian bureaucracy domiciled in the capital who were hostile to any measures leading to a shift of administrative power from Vienna to the provinces. Metternich deprived himself of an alliance with the archdukes by his hostility towards them, motivated by his awareness of their jealousy and potential rivalry, as well as the emperor's distrust of them.

In addition to the mindless opposition, each time he proposed a new reform Metternich had to face a rival for power and influence – first Baldacci, then Wallis, and finally Saurau. Baldacci believed in the soundness of Kaunitz's conception; Wallis, with an odd and rather weak character and of limited intelligence [16], desired loyally to please his emperor; Saurau was a convinced Josephinian centralizer. The objections of the three men to Metternich's proposals had at least the virtue of resting upon recognized principles of government. The man who was now going to oppose him for the next twenty-two years, was a far more unscrupulous enemy because his antagonism stemmed from a selfish lust for power.

[16] Cf. Kübeck, *Tagebücher*, I, 219f., 250f.

CHAPTER IX

ENTER KOLOWRAT

Count Franz Anton Kolowrat-Liebsteinsky was born in 1778 into one of the oldest families of the highest Bohemian nobility. He rose rapidly in the civil service, became governor (*Stadthauptmann*) of Prague in 1807. In that post he first attracted the attention of the emperor by his detailed secret police reports on the activities of Franz's subjects, including the nobility, and on the suppression of Freemasons. As a result he was promoted to Hofrat at the age of thirty and two years later appointed governor (*Oberstburggraf*) of Bohemia. Despite his administrative ability there was much dissatisfaction among his subordinates with his laziness and concern only for those questions that were of personal advantage to him, such as personnel and police matters [1].

In 1826 Count Karl Zichy died and two of his three offices were distributed between Metternich and Kolowrat. The latter was called to Vienna and appointed Staats- und Konferenzminister in charge of section B (internal or political) of the Staatsrat. Metternich succeeded to the presidency of the ministerial conference. But just as his elevation to the office of *Haus-, Hof- und Staatskanzler* five years earlier had not signified any increase of his sphere of action, so his new appointment did not extend his negligible influence on internal affairs. This was due in the first place to the unsatisfactory nature of the conference, largely ignored by the emperor and weakened by the absence of executive ministers, but even more to the arrival of Kolowrat in both conference and Staatsrat [2].

Kolowrat left neither diaries nor memoirs. The only collection of his papers is in the Minister Kolowrat archive in the Haus-, Hof- und Staats-

[1] Springer, *Geschichte*, I, 398f.; Bibl, *Zerfall*, I, 91-94; Friedrich Walter, "Franz Anton Graf Kolowrat-Liebsteinsky", *Neue oesterreichische Biographie ab 1815*, vol. XV (Vienne: Almathea Verlag, 1963), 22.

[2] Beidtel-Huber, *Staatsverwaltung*, 216ff.

archiv in Vienna. Concerned exclusively with official business, they tell little about the minister that is not otherwise available and nothing whatever about the human being. Hence his contemporaries – which means mainly his enemies – provide most of the information about him [3]. The most important source is Kübeck who had known Kolowrat since serving under him in Prague in 1808 [4].

Kolowrat's character was, according to Kübeck, "a strange mixture of enterprising and quiescent weakness". On the one hand his vanity and "burning ambition" to gain exclusive influence on Emperor Franz "and thus to seize the government", resulted in intrigues to place his protegés into leading positions, and even in his bullying the emperor to some degree, once he had reached an influential stature [5]. On the other hand, there were many not very subtle allusions to his laziness, apathy and indolence [6]. Metternich, in a report to Emperor Franz, related Kolowrat's neglect of his work to his health; he referred to his "morbid depression" and added drily "it is the change of seasons" [7].

Metternich always maintained that Kolowrat's bad health influenced his "moral being". Hemorrhoidal attacks, he explained to Ficquelmont and the Tsar, led to irritability, hatred of, and withdrawal from, work [8]. This diagnosis was confirmed by Kolowrat himself who told Kübeck that these attacks made his blood rush to his head and that he then "feared a stroke and did not know what I was doing" [9]. The Prussian minister mentioned chronic abdominal complaints which "affect his mental condition" [10]

[3] No biography has ever been written of this man who exerted such great influence on the Austrian government for twenty-two years. No doubt, this is mainly due to the lack of sources.

[4] Kübeck, *Tagebücher*, I, 249f., 291f. From his first association until the early years of Kolowrat's membership of the government, Kübeck liked and respected him but soon had good reasons to change his attitude. He was one of the earliest victims of Kolowrat's ambition and intrigues which, by 1831, lost him, temporarily, his position of Kabinetts-referent. (Among many references see *Tagebücher*, I, 293, 413, 470, 521, 566, 569, 623, 784, 786). Yet, while this must be borne in mind, Kübeck was a very fair observer who often spoke well of Kolowrat and tried faithfully to cooperate with him (*ibid.*, 623). His strictures on Kolowrat – never strident – have been corroborated by others.

[5] Kübeck, *Tagebücher*, I, 623, 292, 533, 505f., 614.

[6] See for example *ibid.*, 755; Erzherzog Johann's Tagebücher, January 9, 1836 (see below chapter XII).

[7] Vortrag Metternich's, October 30, 1829, HHSA, Staatskanzlei, P.M.

[8] Wertheimer, "Metternich und Staatskonferenz", 50.

[9] Kübeck, *Tagebücher*, I, 737.

[10] Heinrich von Sybel, "Die oesterreichische Staatskonferenz von 1836", *Kleine Historische Schriften* (Stuttgart: Cotta'sche Buchhandlung, 1880), 367.

and the Sardinian envoy similarly wrote of his restless, morose, hypochondriac character influenced by his state of health and, "it is said, by the *époque des équinoxes*" [11]. Hence Kübeck described Kolowrat as "sulking and pouting, always talking contrary to his thoughts", and he more than once deplored his habit of "vilifying things and institutions which are his work" or "which he controls" [12].

If Kolowrat's character was not highly esteemed by his contemporaries, his ability was not rated much better. Metternich found him to be mediocre, observing that he "does not think deeply nor see far ahead. Things are for him as one shows them to him, and he is exceedingly pleased with that" [13]. Stressing that Kolowrat was "born as an instrument but not as a hand" [14], the chancellor thought him unable to "survey" any problem in its entirety, to grasp it or settle it without being confused by incidental matters [15]. Even an opponent of Metternich, the liberal bureaucrat Löwenthal, declared that Kolowrat did "not exceed the ideas or convictions of an able *Kreishauptmann*" (district administrator) [16]. There was, however, little doubt about his masterly skill in political maneuvering which, under the guise of politics, served his personal ambitions.

Kolowrat's politics, like his character, were restless, unsteady, going from one extreme to another. Kübeck noted that he continually pursued "confused aims, rugged plans, disordered projects" and was easily diverted from his goals. He called him "a true political coquette" who was "a puppet of a few intriguers of the common and of the higher sort", seduced by them to actions quite unworthy of his position [17]. Metternich, too, regarded him as a weak "tool in the hands of subordinate flatterers" [18], while Count Carl Clam-Martinitz, Kolowrat's most influential enemy in the Staatsrat, characterized his fickle posturing as that of "a child who plays alternately with different dolls, at one time with the ideal of the almighty minister, at another with the ideal of the independent seigneur" [19]. What Kübeck called a wavering between "acting and standing still, between the existing

[11] Balbo Bertone di Sambuy, *La Politica Estera del Piemonte sotto Carlo Alberto*, ed. Mario degli Alberti (Turin: Fratelli Bocca Librai, 1913-19), I, 188.

[12] Kübeck, *Tagebücher*, I, 755, 769.

[13] Walter, "Metternich-Gervay Briefwechsel", 253.

[14] *NP*, VI, 209.

[15] Wertheimer, "Metternich und Staatskonferenz", 50.

[16] Castle, "Tagebuch Löwenthals", 509.

[17] Kübeck, *Tagebücher*, I, 623, 718, 768.

[18] Wertheimer, "Metternich und Staatskonferenz", 50.

[19] Clam to Metternich, September 28, 1836, HHSA, Staatskanzlei, P.M.

order ... and progress ...", Srbik attributed to an "unstable oscillation" between conservatism and liberalism [20]. It would seem to have been, however, less a case of ideological instability than a tactical and pragmatic maneuvering for political advantage.

Kolowrat regarded himself as an aristocrat and a conservative, defending himself against the general belief that he was a liberal. In a conversation with Kübeck, he explained his ideological disagreement with Metternich as having identical conservative aims but favoring different methods. Analyzing the social and political situation, he rejected Metternich's method of "a forest of bayonets and rigid clinging to the status quo". That, he warned, could only further the cause of revolution by "inciting" both masses and middle class "against our caste". Hence the task was not only to fight false doctrines but also to make timely concessions to improve the welfare of the masses and to absorb "notable" members of the bourgeoisie "into our class" in order to strengthen it with new elements [21].

Metternich was not fooled by Kolowrat's liberal reputation [22]. Nor was Grillparzer who referred contemptuously to him as one "who deports himself as a liberal without anything coming of it" [23]. The popular belief in Kolowrat's liberalism was partly due to his Josephinian anti-clericalism but also because his rivalry with Metternich was attributed to political differences, turning them from rivals into protagonists [24]. Their methods, as Kolowrat correctly said, differed; they were, in fact, so divergent that they quite overshadowed their common aims of "law, order and a powerful government" [25].

Their rivalry first crystallized in Kolowrat's demand to reduce the army in order to improve the financial situation, and in Metternich's insistence to maintain, and even increase, a strong army in order to give the monarchy a powerful position in a frequently tense international situation and to have a ready instrument to fight revolution abroad. In each case political principles reflected a desire to maintain and expand the personal power base of each advocate. Yet reduction of the army was a popular measure with liberals who opposed "anti-liberal armaments since 1830" when they feared intervention against revolutions and urged Austria to confine herself to

[20] Kübeck, *Tagebücher*, I, 551; Srbik, *Metternich*, I, 545.

[21] Kübeck, *Tagebücher*, I, 626f.

[22] Wertheimer, "Metternich und Staatskonferenz", 50.

[23] Franz Grillparzer, *Sämtliche Werke*, ed. Moritz Necker (Leipzig: Hesse & Becker, n.d.) part XVI, 318.

[24] Wertheimer, "Metternich und Staatskonferenz", 111.

[25] Kübeck, *Tagebücher*, I, 627.

"her own interests" [26]. Anyone opposed to armaments was, therefore, ipso facto hailed as a fellow liberal.

Kolowrat also enjoyed a pro-Slav reputation which buttressed that of his liberalism. Some historians have denied his slavophil sentiments as strongly as his alleged liberalism and stressed that the creation of the Bohemian national museum, one of the initiators of the Czech literary renaissance, may have occurred under his governorship but was in no way due to him as he later liked to claim [27]. This may seem a trivial point but it is indicative of what Kübeck called Kolowrat's "duplicity" [28].

A much more significant example of this was his attitude concerning the nobility. To Metternich he described himself as "an aristocrat by birth and conviction" [29]. But to Archduke Carl he denounced his own class, saying that all evil in Austria emanated from the "thoroughly rotten" aristocracy [30]. That was a perfectly respectable view of the nobility, echoed by Archduke Johann who called it "stupid, proud, malicious" [31]. In Kolowrat's case, however, this view seems not to have been based on conviction but on whim or crude opportunism. Kübeck, too, denounced the vicious influence of the magnates [32], and he particularly attacked the "böhmische Nepoten" (Bohemian practitioners of nepotism), the "core of our oligarchic nobility". He accused Kolowrat, "the Bohemian of Bohemians", of inducing the emperor to replace Saurau "by the Moravian-Bohemian Mitrowsky" and Nadasdy, the president of the Hofkammer, "by the Bohemian-Moravian Klebelsberg", a cousin of Kolowrat [33].

It was this partiality on Kolowrat's part for a caste he had pronounced "thoroughly rotten" that provoked Kübeck's charge of duplicity. One immediate consequence of the replacement of efficient and impartial officials by Kolowrat's "creatures" was their prevention of the extension

[26] Grillparzer, *Sämtliche Werke*, part XV, 107. Hence Grillparzer urged improvement of the finances as the first of three measures to save Austria (*ibid.*).

[27] Springer, *Geschichte*, I, 399f.; cf. Kann, *Nationalitätenproblem*, I, 390. This has aroused a historiographical storm in a teacup. Beidtel, explicitly disagreeing with Springer, emphasized Kolowrat's Bohemian nationalism. Bibl – ever ready to find virtue in Metternich's enemies – followed Beidtel. Srbik was silent on the subject, while Walter gives Kolowrat the benefit of the doubt. (Beidtel-Huber, *Staatsverwaltung*, 225-28; Bibl, *Zerfall*, I, 339f.; Walter, "Kolowrat", 26).

[28] Kübeck, *Tagebücher*, I, 520f.

[29] *Ibid.*, 626.

[30] *Ibid.*, 520f.

[31] Sutter, "Erzherzog Johanns Kritik", 202.

[32] See above, p. 5.

[33] Kübeck, *Tagebücher*, I, 333f., 293.

of land-taxes to the Slav provinces [34]. Another, more long-term result of his caste feeling, was the expansion of the system of "supernumerary" officials, used occasionally since 1802, into a regular practice. This favored nobles over commoners through their rapid promotion – without pay in the lower grades – avoiding the years of slow step by step advancement. This practice further demoralized the lower officials, already discouraged by being deprived of all initiative and independence of thought [35].

Kolowrat liked to complain, not without justification, that Metternich made himself "indispensable" to the emperor by constantly facing him with the "spectre of revolution" and by presenting himself as the only man capable of dealing with it [36]. Early in his ministerial career Kolowrat took a leaf out of his rival's book: he, too, was going to be indispensable. His spectre was the desperate condition of the finances from which he would be the only person able to bring deliverance. Hence he immediately set out to acquire an intimate knowledge of the financial administration by cultivating and exploiting its expert officials [37]. It was the beginning of a long and successful campaign.

[34] *Ibid.*

[35] Beidtel-Huber, *Staatsverwaltung*, 228f.; Redlich, *Reichsproblem*, I/1, 74.

[36] Kübeck, *Tagebücher*, I, 621.

[37] *Ibid.*, 292.

CHAPTER X

THE DOUBLE EAGLE

Only five months after appointing Kolowrat to the presidency of the political section of the Staatsrat, the emperor entrusted him with the direction of the financial section as well. Charged also with all personnel matters of the entire Staatsrat [1], he thus rapidly reached the dominant position Zichy had held in that body. With no single overall direction – largely as a result of Metternich's objection – an easy opportunity was created for the man in charge of the two sections concerned with internal affairs to achieve paramount influence over the entire Staatsrat and, through it, over the entire field of internal policy.

Moreover, as a member of the ministerial conference, Kolowrat was able to prevent any potential threat by Metternich to turn the weak conference into a rival instrument of power. He missed none of his chances. As early as 1827 he had his first clash with the chancellor and for the first time made use of the threat of resignation as a form of pressure [2]. What Metternich was to call "the impropriety of the, as it were, periodical entry and withdrawal" recurred twenty times during Emperor Franz's reign alone – an action all the more effective since it was almost completely unknown in pre-March Austria [3].

His first success in his campaign to seize the financial key position [4] came early in 1829. In reports to the emperor Kolowrat drew his attention to the "critical position" of the finances and contrasted Austria's increased state debts to the sounder budgetary policies of other powers during the long years of peace. He demanded an investigation of the situation by experts and a quick implementation of their suggested solutions. Emperor

[1] Srbik, *Metternich*, I, 770 (note 3 to p. 541).

[2] Bibl, *Kaiser Franz*, 322. The cause of their quarrel is not known.

[3] Wertheimer, "Metternich und Staatskonferenz", 50.

[4] Kübeck provides a good survey and analysis of the campaign (*Tagebücher*, I, 292f.).

Franz immediately appointed a finance-commission under Kolowrat's chairmanship to examine public expenditure and revenue, with special attention to internal and external debts. Four months later, in May 1829, Kolowrat was authorized to correspond directly with the Supreme Chancellor and the Minister of Finance on financial matters. At the same time the emperor accorded the commission permanent status [5].

In June Kolowrat was charged with the "immediate direction" of another important commission whose nominal head was the crown prince, Archduke Ferdinand. Its function was to work off arrears accumulated in the emperor's chancellery. It was, apparently, so successful that three years later, when Franz was again overwhelmed by unfinished work, the commission was revived as a "*Comité*", this time with Kolowrat nominally as well as practically in charge. When Ferdinand fell seriously ill, even the crown prince's co-signature was dispensed with [6]. Kolowrat, however, was still not satisfied. A few months later he wanted to change the Comité into what Kübeck called "a kind of sub-government (*Afterregierung*)", ostensibly headed by Ferdinand's younger brother, Archduke Franz Karl, but dominated by Kolowrat. This plan, like so many others among his "disordered projects", was never carried out [7].

Since Stadion's death in 1824 the provisional direction of the ministry of finance had been given to the president of the Hofkammer, Count Michael Nadasdy. Early in 1829 Kolowrat took advantage of this temporary arrangement in his quest for complete financial control. The ministry being clearly an obstacle in his way, he was determined to get rid of it. He complained to the emperor that the present uncertain transitory organization made it difficult for the measures proposed by his financial commission to be put into effect; he, therefore, called for a merger of the ministry with the Hofkammer. Despite Nadasdy's desperate struggle to save the ministry and with it his influential position, Kolowrat managed to persuade the emperor to abolish it in May 1829 [8].

So far all had been smooth sailing for Kolowrat. The first serious storm arose over a conflict with Emperor Franz on the question of discharging state debts. Since the financial commission's proposals for retrenchment had been ignored by the imperial household, the Staatskanzlei, political

[5] Srbik, *Metternich*, I, 541f.; Walter, *Zentralverwaltung*, 147f.

[6] Srbik, *Metternich*, I, 544; Walter, *Zentralverwaltung*, 151f.; Kübeck, *Tagebücher*, I, 560f.

[7] Kübeck, *Tagebücher*, I, 610, 623.

[8] Walter, *Zentralverwaltung*, 260f.

funds and other institutions, Kolowrat intended to reduce expenditure by saving on the payment of state debts. Hence he proposed to grade creditors according to the importance and juridical nature of the debts, but the emperor insisted on treating all creditors alike. The objective merits of Kolowrat's attempts at retrenchment did not conflict with his personal interest. When his policies met with continuous difficulties he resorted to his favorite tactics and submitted his resignation on January 17, 1830 [9].

Emperor Franz immediately turned to Metternich for advice. The chancellor, as has already been noted, used the opportunity to remind the emperor of the continued defects of the government and necessity of reform. In a matter-of-fact tone he summarized his often repeated points without much hope of success [10]. Kolowrat, he conceded, had some justification for his complaints but he was only "fighting with symptoms". He regarded him as "ill" and saw his resignation as "the repeated product of a morbidly excited disposition". Nevertheless, he advised the emperor to make another attempt to retain Kolowrat because "*a minister can go but a monarch must remain – hence there is nothing to be gained by going*". Kolowrat, Metternich charged, while originally agreeing with him on the need to keep government and administration apart, had since violated this precept and had now "substituted despair for the search for improvement". Hence Metternich proposed to talk to him, to find out "what he really thought and wanted" and to "demonstrate to him" where he was in error.

The day after that discussion had taken place, Kolowrat, in a letter to Metternich [11], graciously agreed, because of his "close attachment to the all-highest person of the emperor", to carry on provisionally with the direction of financial affairs "until a better method was discovered". When Metternich who had taken the resignation seriously reported his success to the emperor, Franz added a comment to the report that he "could not refrain from disclosing that I would presumably not have been able to preserve the Austrian state if I had had or still have only such servants as Count Kolowrat" [12].

Kübeck noted in his diary that Metternich, "indisputably generous and conciliatory", had moved to retain Kolowrat "whom he no longer feared" [13]. If Metternich's move was generous, it was also one of the biggest mistakes

[9] Srbik, *Metternich*, I, 542; Walter, *Zentralverwaltung*, 148.

[10] Vortrag Metternich's, January 19, 1830, HHSA, Staatskanzlei, P.M. See above p. 50.

[11] Kolowrat to Metternich, 21 January, 1830, *ibid.*

[12] Vortrag Metternich's, 20 January, 1830, *ibid.*

[13] Kübeck, *Tagebücher*, I, 293.

of his life. Five and six years later he was to have two more opportunities to get rid of Kolowrat but, although he seized them, he was unsuccessful because his rival had grown too strong. Now, in 1830, there was still a genuine chance. By not taking it he allowed Kolowrat to recover and to proceed from strength to strength.

Kolowrat quickly recaptured Emperor Franz's favor by presenting in August 1830, "for the first time in decades", as he proudly proclaimed, a balanced budget which even produced a small surplus. The grateful emperor admitted his need for Kolowrat's "help, especially to put the various branches of the administration in order as well as to settle the remaining financial matters". When the minister advised Franz on the investment of his private fortune with profitable results [14], he was rewarded with the replacement of Saurau and Nadasdy by his protegés [15]. Nadasdy, appointed minister, replaced Kolowrat as head of the financial section of the Staatsrat. That meant, however, no diminution of the latter's power since his financial commission had taken over all important financial questions from section C [16].

Kolowrat was in a good position to resist Metternich's policy of rearmament and armed intervention when the July Revolution, the risings in Modena, Parma and the Papal States, and the international tension of the next few years threatened Austria's financial equilibrium once more. It was a clash of incompatible political principles [17]. Kolowrat opposed the chancellor's primacy of foreign policy, while Metternich, in its name, made excessive demands on Austria's economic power. Yet, due to the emperor's faith in a strong army as an instrument against the revolution and as a guarantee of an influential position for Austria, Kolowrat was not very successful. He complained to Kübeck that when he had challenged the emperor and warned that putting the army on a war footing and continuous loans would lead to bankruptcy, Franz had answered "indifferently: 'What does it matter? Bankruptcy is a tax like any other. One must simply see to it that everybody loses in equal proportion, in the manner in which an honest merchant fails in business' " [18].

During this period of the early thirties another dangerous enemy of Metternich rose to prominence by intriguing with, and sometimes against,

[14] August Fournier, "Graf Kolowrat und die oesterreichische Staatskonferenz in 1836", *Historische Studien und Skizzen*, 3. Reihe (Vienna: Tempsky, 1912), 267f.

[15] See above p. 58.

[16] Walter, *Zentralverwaltung*, 151.

[17] Kübeck, *Tagebücher*, I, 533-35.

[18] *Ibid.*, 593.

Kolowrat to become president of the Hofkammer. Peter Josef von Eichhoff, a career official born in the Rhineland, was appointed vice-president of the Hofkammer in 1831 at Kolowrat's recommendation in order to give professional support to the newly appointed president, Kolowrat's cousin Count Franz Klebelsberg, whose incompetence threatened to become a public scandal [19]. From the beginning the relationship between Eichhoff and Kolowrat was ambiguous. Kübeck concluded that Eichhoff obtained the vice-presidency by blackmailing Kolowrat over Klebelsberg's position. Two of Kolowrat's early victims agreed with this view of Eichhoff's dominant position. Nadasdy spoke of his "incredible influence over Kolowrat" whom he "guided" in his own "personal interest", while the Hofkanzler Franz von Pillersdorf regarded the minister as "the prey of impertinent plotters", by which Kübeck understood him to mean Eichhoff and Klebelsberg [20].

Three or four years later the situation was still not clear. Metternich referred to Eichhoff as "a born tyrant" and asserted that "he terrorizes Count Kolowrat" [21]. When Eichhoff was promoted to Hofkammerpräsident in 1835 [22] Kübeck used the occasion to fulminate against the character of this "self-made foreigner (*Roturier*)"

> who had served hardly ten years since becoming a copyist, who has never done anything in any branch, who, without any wealth, has bought two estates in Moravia since his four or five years with the financial service.

Kübeck may not even have exaggerated. In any case, the tone of jealousy should not be allowed to detract from the truth, particularly of his conclusion that the promotion "proved the power and the influence of [Kolowrat] whose creature Eichhoff is" [23]. Three months later Kübeck wondered which of the two was "the dependent one" [24]. As late as 1838 Kübeck still found that Kolowrat, "incurable in his conceit, does not know, does not devine, that he is a tool of an intriguing rabble" [25]. Clam-Martinitz even

[19] *Ibid.*, 533, 436f.

[20] *Ibid.*, 533, 569, 551.

[21] *NP*, VI, 211, 213.

[22] The date of Eichhoff's appointment to the presidency of the Hofkammer is disputed. Fournier ("Kolowrat und Staatskonferenz", 269) gives it as November 1834, which is accepted by Srbik (*Metternich*, I, 544) and repeated by Walter (*Zentralverwaltung*, 152). Kübeck (*Tagebücher*, I, 701) dates it October 20, 1835.

[23] Kübeck, *Tagebücher*, I, 701.

[24] *Ibid.*, 715. The diary refers to "E. o. K.".

[25] *Ibid.*, 778.

spoke of a "Eichhoffian liberal party" which needed Kolowrat's "name for its plans, and his power for its interests" [26].

Whatever the true nature of their relationship, it is clear that Eichhoff's close association with Kolowrat was of advantage to both. In a letter to Metternich during the cabinet crisis of 1836, Eichhoff claimed that Franz had ordered him two years earlier to discuss all important financial matters with Kolowrat and had authorized him, if he obtained the minister's agreement, to act without first getting the emperor's permission in all cases where publicity might be harmful, even if his official field of competence was thereby exceeded [27]. He may, of course, have strayed beyond the limits of truth since his letter was a move in a desperate power struggle. In any case his increasingly powerful position and alliance with Kolowrat supported the latter in his rivalry with Metternich.

A ministerial conference, so often and convincingly advocated by Metternich, could never even begin to function as the highest governmental organ he had envisaged, because, after 1830, Metternich was the only minister with a department and with executive powers. Some sort of conference did exist, however, and met periodically. It was variously entitled "select (*engste*)" or "secret" conference; its permanent members consisted of its president, Metternich, of Kolowrat, and of Sedlnitzky, the president of the Polizeihofstelle, with Hofrat Josef von Gervay keeping the minutes. "Sedlnitzky was there", as Kübeck acidly noted, "quia tres faciunt consilium". Metternich gradually managed to dominate the conference with the aid of non-permanent members such as the Hungarian Hofkanzler, and to use it as a counterweight to the Staatsrat in which Kolowrat held the commanding position. The conference never achieved a firm constitutional status mainly because of the emperor's distrust, and its influence fluctuated according to the political fortunes of its two principal members [28].

Kolowrat's tactics against Metternich included a sustained affort to undermine Emperor Franz's confidence in his chancellor through aspersions upon the latter's financially ruinous policies and politically dangerous unpopularity. He combined his insidious attempts to cripple the conference with proposals to reform the Staatsrat designed to place him into a more powerful position against Metternich. The two main purposes of his Staatsrat plans seem to have been an evasion of the sectional division and the elimination of the Hungarian chancellor whose independent spirit and

[26] Clam to Metternich, September 28, 1836, HHSA, Staatskanzlei, P.M.

[27] Eichhoff to Metternich, October 20, 1836, HHSA, Staatsrat Praes., Kart. 4.

[28] Hock-Bidermann, *Staatsrat*, 672f.; Kübeck, *Tagebücher*, I, 299, 357, 455f., 467, 469f.

cooperation with Metternich threatened his schemes. Metternich countered these moves in a conciliatory manner by appearing to "initiate his rival in his secrets in order to render him harmless". Until Emperor Franz's death Metternich constantly underestimated his opponent's political skill, ruthlessness and determination [29].

The rivalry did not displease the emperor. He was quite happy to have two ministers at the head of the government, competing for his favor, and to be able to keep the balance between them [30]. If the motto "divide and rule" suited his absolutist principle, it was yet another nail in the coffin of effective government. In Fieldmarshal Count Bellegarde's words, "Metternich and Kolowrat form the imperial eagle. One head looks to the right, the other to the left" [31]. It was a case where two heads were not better than one.

Metternich's lack of influence in internal matters was perhaps as much due to the emperor's jealous preservation of his own chosen sphere of action, as to the neglect of Austria's internal problems, considered to be petty, by "a world-governing statesman", as Kübeck put it [32]. While blaming Metternich for dominating Franz in "a kind of regency", Kolowrat took advantage of this situation to aim, as Kübeck accused him, at absolute power. By referring in 1832 to "Kolowrat's plan to wring the sceptre from the emperor's hand and to establish a camarilla rule under the all-highest name", Kübeck probably meant the abortive plan to dominate the government through a committee headed by Archduke Franz Karl [33].

Aging and in bad health, the emperor became increasingly dependent upon Kolowrat and, to some degree, diffident in his presence. Kübeck reports two revealing incidents. During a conference attended by himself, Kolowrat and the emperor, the minister insisted on some point against Franz's opposition. The latter, apparently, gave way, signed Kolowrat's order and, at the same time, made a note on a piece of paper. Shortly thereafter he left the room "as if he had to ease his nature" but soon returned. Kübeck learned afterwards from the Kabinetts-Direktor to whom the emperor had given the paper that it had countermanded the order Franz had conceded to Kolowrat [34].

[29] Kübeck, *Tagebücher*, I, 469f., 593, 505f., 299.
[30] *Ibid.*, 585, 767.
[31] Corti, *Metternich*, II, 365. Cf. Kübeck, *Tagebücher*, I, 678.
[32] Srbik, *Metternich*, I, 453; Kübeck, *Tagebücher*, I, 623, 440.
[33] Kübeck, *Tagebücher*, I, 592, 560, 610.
[34] *Ibid.*, 614.

Three months later, irritated by his constant "suppression and displacement" on the part of Kolowrat, Kübeck asked the emperor to explain the apparent loss of favor and confidence. Franz answered graciously that "he had nothing whatever against" him and explained that Kübeck was no longer allowed to report alone to the emperor but only in Kolowrat's presence only because the minister had requested it. "Don't worry", Emperor Franz promised Kübeck, "This will change again". Kolowrat was going to leave in the autumn to spend the winter in Italy. "Then we shall fully resume our former relationship" [35].

It is therefore not surprising that Kolowrat reached a position described as "without any actual institution, a kind of Prime Minister" [36]. Similarly, Kolowrat's office, informally known as "*Ministerial-Department*", was "considered, not unjustly, as a kind of *Ministerpräsidium*" [37]. All that Metternich could do to oppose this victorious advance was to obtain, after an embarrassing and pathetic quarrel of rank with the Lord High Steward, from an emperor reluctant to abandon tradition, the empty formality of precedence over all other officials [38].

[35] *Ibid.*, 623f.; cf. *ibid.*, 521.

[36] Srbik, *Metternich*, I, 544. Cf. the baseless assertion by Constantin de Grunwald that until Emperor Franz's death Metternich "managed to stamp every branch of the administration with his own personality: he enjoyed the privileges of a Prime Minister without being called upon to bear official responsibility". (*Metternich* [London: Falcon Press, 1953], 255f.).

[37] Fournier, "Kolowrat und Staatskonferenz", 269.

[38] Kübeck, *Tagebücher*, I, 670.

CHAPTER XI

THE SUCCESSION QUESTION

Crown Prince Ferdinand, Emperor Franz's older son, was amiable, well-meaning, epileptic and weakminded. Born in 1793, his mental and physical incapacity to rule was obvious since his childhood. When he recovered from a severe illness in 1832 after having been given up by his doctors, the court was not pleased since his death would have solved many future difficulties. His physician in ordinary declined credit for saving Ferdinand with the words "doctors and medicine have done nothing here. Only the good luck (*Sauglück*) of this man, the King, has saved him once again" [1].

Naturally there had been many suggestions to exclude Ferdinand from the succession, starting with the advice of the Archbishop of Vienna in 1812 that Emperor Franz should declare his son unfit to rule [2]. But the emperor persistently refused to change the succession and Metternich supported his refusal. The chancellor's motives were complex. In the first place, though he was not quite the "Don Quixote of legitimism" of Grillparzer's poem [3], as the cases of Napoleon and Murat had proven, his principles would not allow a modification of the dynastic right of succession even if that meant "an absolute monarchy without a monarch", as Kübeck jeered [4]. Then there was the apprehension of legal disputes with Hungary over the admissibility of a regency and the choice of a regent or regency council. Moreover, in any kind of regency the Hungarian diet could not be prevented from playing an important part and all the advantages gained by Ferdinand's coronation in 1830 would thus be lost [5].

[1] Kübeck, *Tagebücher*, I, 605, 609f. Since his coronation as King of Hungary in 1830, Ferdinand used the title of King.

[2] Grunwald, *Metternich*, 251.

[3] "Grabschrift", *Sämtliche Werke*, part 2, 141.

[4] Srbik, *Metternich*, I, 552; Kübeck, *Tagebücher*, I, 679.

[5] Springer, *Geschichte*, I, 443f.

Finally there was the problem of the archdukes. Any change in the succession was likely to set ablaze the smouldering embers of their rivalries and factions if only in a competition to become regent. Metternich's ambition could not tolerate any concessions to Carl and Johann, the two ablest of the princes, who had hitherto been prevented by Franz from taking any active part in politics [6].

Hence Metternich had always been an advocate of a veiled regency [7]. Years later he described to Hartig how he had pleaded with Emperor Franz, after the latter's recovery from a dangerous illness in 1826, "to secure the means to govern for his successor". The only way was "to erect a governmental machine" with whose aid even Ferdinand could rule [8]. Thus one aspect of Metternich's reform policy was the desire to create a government sufficiently strong and effective to dispense with imperial tutelage. After Emperor Franz's death, Metternich would be the power behind the throne, operating from the basis of his presidency of a greatly strengthened ministerial conference. The trouble was that it was not possible to create such a strong government during Franz's lifetime; after his death it was too late. And there was always Kolowrat.

In the last years of Franz's reign Kolowrat vaccilated between two policies, cooperation with Metternich or exclusive power for himself. In November 1833 he decided on a rapprochement with the chancellor "in view of the increasing weakness of the emperor", as he explained. His aim was "to divide the government with him" [9]. Later, reviving the plan of coming to power under Archduke Franz Karl's nominal rule, he favored the scheme of Archduchess Sophie, Franz Karl's wife. Sophie, a Bavarian princess and sister of the Empress Caroline Augusta, wanted to eliminate Ferdinand from the succession and give it to his brother, her husband. Her ambition should not be allowed to detract from the rationality and relative simplicity of this plan. She never quite forgave Metternich for rejecting it; she was to remember her resentment in March 1848. Two years later, with her son Franz Josef instead of her husband on the throne, she

[6] Srbik, *Metternich,* I, 552; II, 3.

[7] The French chargé d'affaires in Munich reported in 1826 that Metternich's plan to persuade Ferdinand to renounce the throne in favor of his brother had failed and that the chancellor intended to resign upon Franz's death because his enemies were getting too powerful. (Anton Chroust, ed., *Gesandschaftsberichte aus München 1814-48,* part I, vol. II [Munich: *Kommission für bayerische Landesgeschichte,* 1935], 17). Nowhere else is there any mention of this plan.

[8] *Metternich-Hartig Briefwechsel,* 43.

[9] Kübeck, *Tagebücher,* I, 647.

told Princess Melanie Metternich, the chancellor's third wife, that she still reproached her husband with wanting "an impossible thing: to conduct the monarchy without an emperor and with an imbecile (*Trottel*) as representative of the crown" [10].

When Sophie's opposition to Metternich's legitimist policy proved unavailing, Kolowrat again approached the chancellor. In 1848 Metternich told the diplomat Alexander von Hübner how Kolowrat, a few days before Franz's death, suggested "to divide the power with me. 'You retain', he told me, 'the external and I take the internal'. I replied with some sarcastic remark, whereupon he exclaimed: 'Well then, things remain as they were!' " [11].

When Emperor Franz fell ill at the end of February 1835 and it was soon clear that the end was near, Metternich was prepared. He had discussed the details of his last directions with the emperor for some time, and in accordance with his instructions Friedrich Gentz had drawn up a draft for a political testament several years earlier [12]. During the last days of Franz's illness Metternich prepared another draft, on church policy, with the aid of Franz's confessor. It enjoined Ferdinand to continue the "work of correction and modification" of the Josephinian church law in conformity with the Pope's wishes. Emperor Franz, fully conscious, dictated his political testament as two letters to his son, guided by these and other drafts, and signed them on February 28 [13].

In the second letter the emperor asked his son not to "disturb" the "foundation of the edifice of the state" and to remain faithful to his father's principles. "Reign and change nothing" – that might have been Franz's motto too, with the difference that he had ruled. Archduke Ludwig was to be Ferdinand's closest adviser: "Give [him] ... your fullest confidence. Seek his advice in all important internal questions". Ferdinand was also urged to trust in Metternich, "my most faithful servant and friend", and not to come to any decision "in public and personnel matters" without having "heard" him [14].

Metternich's last draft for the political letter, in his own hand and based on Gentz's, was more detailed than the final testament signed by the em-

[10] Quoted in Schlitter, *Vormärz*, IV, 122. This passage from Melanie's diary is omitted in *NP*, VIII.

[11] Hübner, *Ein Jahr*, 14.

[12] Bibl, *Zerfall*, I, 386f.

[13] Srbik, *Metternich*, I, 554f.

[14] Text of political (not religious or private) part of testament printed in *NP*, V, 651 and Kübeck, *Tagebücher*, I, 675f.

peror. It made no reference at all to either Ludwig or Metternich, and the chancellor, modestly, left an open space for the name of the adviser to be inserted by Emperor Franz [15]. The emperor's additions and alterations – even about Ludwig – did not change the essential fact that Metternich had finally arrived at his goal. A unified government under his influence and direction was to be established, with the incapacitated Ferdinand reigning and leaving all change and reform as well as governing to his chancellor. Of the archdukes only Ludwig, the most ineffectual and youngest but one of Franz's eight brothers [16] who had often deputized for the emperor in the past, had a share in the government.

Nevertheless, Princess Melanie, undoubtedly reflecting her husband's thoughts, worried the day after Franz's death that "one must see to it that the emperor [Ferdinand] does not walk into the trap" of the more senior and abler of the archdukes [17]. Most important of all, Kolowrat's name was not even mentioned in the political testament. It only appeared in the private will, signed at the same time, where the emperor thanked him for having restored order to his private affairs [18]. Kolowrat's power seemed at last to have been eliminated.

Emperor Franz died early on March 2, 1835. The next day Kolowrat, talking to Kübeck, shed "Bohemian tears" and, unaware of the existence of the testament, still spoke about dividing power with Metternich. He now proposed to use Ludwig as a "shield" against the nobility and the archdukes [19]. One day later, on March 4, Kolowrat learned of the testament and immediately fought back. Unfortunately nothing is known about the decisive confrontation of that day except Kübeck's terse account of what Kolowrat told him on the same afternoon. The minister declared that he had just frustrated Metternich's attempt "to seize the cabinet". As so often before Kolowrat had threatened to "leave Vienna at once and retire to his estates". Metternich gave in [20].

[15] For details of origin, signing and genuineness of the testament see Srbik's long footnote (*Metternich*, I, 772f.) and Fritz von Reinöhl, "Das politische Vermächtnis des Kaiser Franz I", *Historische Blätter*, 7. Heft (1937), 71-78. Metternich's draft is unaccountably missing from HHSA, Staatskanzlei, Acta Secreta 1835, No. 480.

[16] Ludwig is often referred to as the youngest of the brothers (e.g. Walter, *Zentralverwaltung*, 165), forgetting Rudolf, Archbishop of Olmütz.

[17] Corti, *Metternich*, II, 370. Cf. the vaguer wording in *NP*, V, 627.

[18] Bibl, *Kaiser Franz*, 389; Srbik, *Metternich*, I, 773 (note 1 to p. 555).

[19] Kübeck, *Tagebücher*, I, 677.

[20] *Ibid.*, 678.

He neither faced Kolowrat with the alternatives of obeying Franz's last will or leaving the imperial service, nor did he counter with the threat of his own resignation, an almost irresistible form of pressure in view of its international significance. Srbik speculates on his reasons for lacking confidence in his own strong position and on the motives which might explain why "the soft and despondent part of his nature prevailed". Unwillingness to face the hatred of a defeated rival, a struggle with the archdukes or the unpopularity of dismissing the "liberal" Kolowrat – all may have played a part [21]. Metternich himself is silent on this question, as is his wife's diary.

The two ministers agreed to invite Archduke Ludwig to exercise a kind of unofficial regency, unavowed and secret to the public [22]. Ludwig accepted with a promise to protect them against other members of the imperial family [23]. Thus was established what Metternich called "the Trinity" [24] that was to last thirteen years.

The chancellor hastened to assure the world, at home and abroad, that all was well and nothing had really changed. "Archduke Ludwig, I, and Count Kolowrat stand united, one for all and all for one", he wrote both to Count Joachim Münch, the Austrian ambassador to the Frankfurt Bundestag, and to Archduke Ferdinand, cousin of Ludwig and governor of Transylvania. Modifying this beautiful picture, he added to Münch that Ludwig's role was to take care of the "rubbish" (*Quark* – a favorite expression of Metternich) such as giving audiences. To Archduke Ferdinand he gave an optimistic account of increased government efficiency:

> The conference remains, as hitherto, the highest ostensible authority; the Hofstellen will get the wider sphere of activity that the late emperor should have given them. The Staatsrat remains as it is but will receive less nonsense [25].

The new emperor hardly understood a word of what his ministers or Staatsräte told him. He addressed them in words drilled into him and was always ready to sign anything placed before him. Kübeck called the ministerial handling of Ferdinand a "conjuring trick" or "deception and fraud" [26]. In order to hide the emperor's true nature as far and as long as possible,

[21] Srbik, *Metternich*, II, 4.

[22] One reason for secrecy was the threat of constitutional complications in Hungary.

[23] Kübeck, *Tagebücher*, I, 678.

[24] Metternich to Kolowrat, November 1, 1837, HHSA, Praes., Kart. 4.

[25] Metternich to Münch, March 7; to Ferdinand, March 20, 1835, HHSA, Kabinettarchiv, Konferenzakten.

[26] Kübeck, *Tagebücher*, I, 678f.

it was necessary to watch him closely at public functions [27], otherwise he was liable to do things like asking the Belgian minister to express his regret over the Prince's of Orange illness to King Leopold [28].

Important decisions were taken in the name of a fiction, "the will of the imperial family", in order to satisfy the public [29]. But if Ferdinand did not count for anything, neither was the empress, Maria Anna of Savoy, of much help. Claim-Martinitz called her a "truthful and kind-hearted nun", while Archduke Johann deplored that she could not be of much use to her husband. "A good woman, limited by her monastic-Italian upbringing, pious, unacquainted with the world – what council can she give?" [30]. Archduke Franz Karl, though not afflicted by the mental or physical defects of his brother, had such an insignificant personality that his wife soon transferred her ambitions from him to their son Franz, the future Emperor Franz-Josef.

With Archdukes Carl and Johann in enforced and resentful retirement away from Vienna, and with those archdukes who were heads of provincial administrations – Josef in Hungary, Rainer in Lombardo-Venetia, Max in Galicia, and Ferdinand in Transylvania – acquiescing in the regency arrangements, there were only two persons at court who mattered. Ludwig and Sophie alone, the French ambassador found, represented that elusive will of the imperial family. The question was, which of the two influenced the other. In view of the "phlegmatic and sleepy" appearance of one, and the "forever excited and fierce" personality of the other, the ambassador thought it unlikely that the initiative belonged to Ludwig [31]. "The only man at court", was the Prussian minister's view of Sophie [32].

Ludwig resembled Emperor Franz in his mediocrity and dullness. Like his brother, he abhorred oral discussions and permitted the reintroduction of the misuse of written reports [33]. Unlike Franz, however, he did not much care for written reports either [34]. He was afraid of responsibility and deci-

[27] *Ibid.*, 685f.

[28] Louis de Sainte-Aulaire, "Souvenirs de mon Ambassade à Vienne", *La Revue de Paris*, XXXI (December 1924), 793; Sambuy, *La Politica Estera*, I, 64.

[29] Sainte-Aulaire, *Souvenirs*, 146f.

[30] Clam to Metternich, August 15, 1836, HHSA, Staatskanzlei, K; Erzherzog Johann, Tagebücher, March 3, 1835.

[31] Sainte-Aulaire, *Souvenirs*, 339. Cf. Wertheimer, "Metternich und Staatskonferenz", 116, on Sophie's influence on Ludwig.

[32] Bibl, *Zerfall*, II, 39.

[33] Hartig, *Genesis*, 37.

[34] Metternich tried to keep letters to Ludwig "as short as possible lest he be bored". (*NP*, VI, 210).

sions. "*Liegen lassen ist die beste Erledigung* (postpone it, that is the best way to settle things)", was his favorite saying [35]. His brother Johann took a charitable view, reproaching him only for undertaking too little "from too much modesty" [36]; Kolowrat, less kindly, called him "nothing but a busy Hofrat" [37]; while Metternich regretted that "he was not able to rise to the position of a regent" [38]. Ludwig would probably have agreed with the chancellor. In 1837 he told Clam-Martinitz frankly, "the situation is new for me and I cannot quite get reconciled to it. All my life I have been used to obey and I prefer nothing more than to have someone above me" [39].

Metternich seemed in an optimistic mood during the first few weeks of the new reign. He was apparently reconciled to his abandonment of Franz's testament and was ready to make the best of the new situation. In a private letter to Ficquelmont in April 1835, he expressed his satisfaction at not having lost his head during the crisis. He admitted that "one man cannot do everything" and that he needed the aid of others. But he was confident of the future and of his ability to guide the new emperor "in the right direction" [40].

Kübeck's judgment of the situation was, therefore, realistic, if harsh. Less than two weeks after Franz's death he predicted that Metternich and Kolowrat would run the government, make all appointments and dish out business to the Staatsrat "piecemeal, as to a secretariat", while believing it possible to "hide their arbitrary power from the world" [41]. Both Metternich's and Kübeck's expectations depended on the unity of the trinity or, as Kolowrat rightly preferred to call it, of "the Duumvires" [42].

[35] Hübner, *Ein Jahr*, 8; Sambuy, *La Politica Estera*, I, 159.

[36] Erzherzog Johann, Tagebücher, January 9, 1836. Churchill's famous epigram about Attlee is much more appropriate here.

[37] Corti, *Metternich*, II, 369.

[38] *NP*, VII, 618.

[39] Clam to Metternich, August 2, 1837, HHSA, Staatskanzlei, K.

[40] *NP*, VI, 7f.

[41] Kübeck, *Tagebücher*, I, 679.

[42] *Ibid.*, 678.

CHAPTER XII

THE GOVERNMENT OF THE DALAI LAMA

Austria was ruled by 30 persons, according to the current joke: Ludwig, Metternich and Kolowrat made 3, plus a zero for Emperor Ferdinand [1]. The trouble with the new government was not only a question of who or how many ruled, but *how* they ruled. To Kolowrat it was a "government of the Dalai Lama", with Ferdinand representing the remote and mystic ruler who was often a child, and the ministers ruling as "his priests" [2]. What was worse, two of the abuses of the previous reign were soon rampant again among high government leaders: preoccupation with trivialities on the one hand, disunity, conflict and rivalry on the other. A characteristic example of the first is the minutes of a conference session devoted to one subject only. The document is entitled:

Conferenz-Protokoll, September 16, 1835

Report by the royal-Hungarian Hofkanzler, announcing that Franz Schedel has been elected secretary of the Hungarian learned society [3].

Archduke Johann described the disunity of the government after a Christmas visit to Vienna:

Everywhere self-seeking and so few with quiet self-denial. ... That much is certain, that all are against each other, that some truth is at the bottom of all the talk that sometimes amounts to slander.

Most of the talk focused on the two chief ministers. The emperor's personal physician, Staatsrat Andreas von Stifft and Count Ludwig Taaffe, president of the Oberste Justizstelle, for example, bitterly denounced Kolowrat, his laziness, his limited talent and the fact that he was a tool of others. They demanded a curtailment of his powers and complained that Metternich

[1] Sambuy, *La Politica Estera*, I, 170.

[2] Kübeck, *Tagebücher*, I, 679.

[3] HHSA, Kabinettarchiv, Konferenzakten, No. 1733, 1835.

made light of everything. The chancellor, Johann noted, was blamed for knowing all about Kolowrat, for being aware of what was going on and yet not interfering in the mistaken belief that he could best step in when things became worst [4].

It is instructive to follow the development of the most acute political observer's thinking during the first two years of the new reign. For several months Kübeck bitterly attacked both ministers for "usurping power" and pursuing their own personal interests. In his strongest denouncement he called them an "usurping camarilla ... without interest for the nation or the state" [5]. Slowly, however, his diary entries began to differentiate between the characters, abilities and objectives of the two men. Kolowrat does not seem to have made a secret of his ambitions. When Clam-Martinitz defined Kolowrat's "ideal" to Metternich as "an unrestrained Direktorial-Minister for internal and financial matters", he seemed to quote Kolowrat himself [6].

Once Kübeck realized that Kolowrat's "craving for power more and more bursts forth into arbitrary actions" [7], he singled him out for attack. He became increasingly contemptuous of the minister's character – calling him liar, intriguer and "homunculus" [8] – and finally drew up a balanced judgment of the two co-regents. On the one side Metternich: "magnanimous, intelligent, clear-sighted"; called upon "too late to participate in the direction of internal affairs, he cannot quite master them. ... Opposite him stands Kolowrat who cannot rise above being governor of Bohemia", who carries on his business with a "veneer of routine, without culture, without principles, without positive knowledge" [9].

The political situation gradually polarized into two opposing and increasingly hostile factions. One side was led by Kolowrat and Hofkammerpräsident Eichhoff, "the wirepuller (*faiseur*)", as Kübeck called him [10]; the other Metternich [11] and Clam-Martinitz. General Clam, who considered himself a pupil of Metternich and shared most of his political views, had been appointed *Generaladjutant* to Ferdinand on the day of the emperor's

[4] Erzherzog Johann, Tagebücher, January 9, 1836.

[5] Kübeck, *Tagebücher*, I, 697, 693, 704, 721.

[6] Clam to Metternich, September 28, 1836, HHSA, Staatskanzlei, P.M. Clam put the phrase in quotation marks and underlined it.

[7] Kübeck, *Tagebücher*, I, 684.

[8] *Ibid.*, 717, 718, 735, 737, 758f.

[9] *Ibid.*, 767f.

[10] *Ibid.*, 520.

[11] Metternich disliked the idea of factions or parties. "I do not want a Metternich party", he told Clam (Clam to Metternich, August 2, 1837, HHSA, Staatskanzlei, K.). Cf. Kübeck, *Tagebücher*, I, 775.

accession. In February 1836 he was made head of the military section of the Staatsrat. The combination of these two offices – a seat in the government and immediate access to the emperor – made him virtually Minister of War and a most valuable ally of Metternich [12].

As Kübeck was rapidly gaining influence through ability and character, both factions wooed him. While keeping his independence [13], he inclined towards Metternich and proved to be a useful adviser to the chancellor. As an expert in financial and economic subjects, he supplied Metternich with facts and figures, was frequently invited to attend the Staatskonferenz and often supported the chancellor on economic and other policies [14].

Metternich was aware that he had to strengthen his position. If he could prove to the world that he was firmly in control of Austria's government, the heightened prestige abroad would reinforce his influence at home. An opportunity was provided by the forthcoming unveiling in northern Bohemia of a Russian monument to the allied victory at Kulm in 1813. Two years earlier, when the three Eastern courts had met nearby to sign the agreements of Münchengrätz, the Tsar had promised Emperor Franz to "protect his weak successor" [15]. Now the courts of Austria, Prussia and Russia were to meet again, to renew their somewhat shaky friendship and profess their solidarity, to introduce the new Austrian emperor to his fellow monarchs, and to demonstrate the unity of the Habsburg family and their confidence in the chancellor [16].

The meeting at Teplitz in October 1835 was a great success for Metternich. Archdukes Carl and Johann lent luster to the court without detracting from Metternich's prestige. The Tsar was appalled by Ferdinand's condition which he found even worse than anticipated [17]. "Your situation is unique in history", he told Kolowrat; "I am amazed that things are with you as they are" [18]. Tsar Nicholas, who two years earlier had written to his wife that each time he saw Metternich he begged God to protect him from the devil [19], now told the chancellor, "keep well, for you are our key-stone.

[12] Eduard Wertheimer, "Clam-Martinitz", *Allgemeine Deutsche Biographie*, Nachträge, XLVII, 490-96.

[13] Kübeck, *Tagebücher*, I, 761.

[14] Adolf Beer, "Kübeck und Metternich", 3.

[15] Theodor Schiemann, *Geschichte Russlands unter Kaiser Nikolaus I* (Berlin: Reimer, 1913), III, 237f.

[16] Kübeck, *Tagebücher*, I, 697f.

[17] Schiemann, *Geschichte Russlands*, III, 271.

[18] Kübeck, *Tagebücher*, I, 700.

[19] Schiemann, *Geschichte Russlands*, III, 235.

As long as the arches do not complain about the key ... the building will not crumble" [20]. That, at least, is what Metternich triumphantly wrote to his wife. But the Tsar had endorsed his rival as well by telling Kolowrat (according to Kolowrat), "as long as your respective positions do not change, one can trust Austria" [21]. Thus while Teplitz enhanced Metternich's prestige abroad it hardly affected the domestic political situation.

One immediate consequence of Teplitz was Archduke Carl's request of the emperor to be made generalissimo of the army. Attributing the decline of unity and discipline in the army to the fact that the army commander was not simultaneously the emperor's closest military adviser, he proposed a return to the arrangement of 1805-08 when he had successfully combined both positions [22]. Kübeck has suggested plausibly that Carl had been "enticed" to Teplitz by a promise of an influential position [23]. If the promise had been made, it was never meant to be kept.

For a quarter of a century the archduke and Metternich had been enemies, ever since Carl had accused Stadion and Metternich of starting the war of 1809 which he had opposed. Partly due to Metternich, the lost war had cost him the command of the army. He had also disagreed with the Foreign Minister on the use of popular forces, first against Napoleon, and later to strengthen the country economically and politically [24]. Metternich, on his part, had blamed Carl for giving up prematurely at Wagram and for concluding shortly afterwards an armistice with Napoleon, wrongly and without political authorization. Carl's refusal in 1812 to take command of the Austrian auxiliary corps against Russia in accordance with Napoleon's request further estranged Metternich and annoyed Emperor Franz [25]. As a result, Metternich frustrated Carl's planned marriage to the Tsar's sister-in-law, though political motives were also involved [26].

When war threatened in France and Italy in 1831, the chancellor opposed Franz's wish to have Carl lead the army. But Carl in any event opposed his

[20] *NP*, VI, 81.

[21] Kübeck, *Tagebücher*, I, 700.

[22] Carl's note to Ferdinand, October 21, 1835, printed in Kübeck, *Tagebücher*, I, 705-07 and in Oskar Criste, *Erzherzog Carl von Oesterreich* (Vienna: Braumüller, 1912), III, 456-58. On the weakness of the Austrian army, see Gunther E. Rothenberg, "The Austrian Army in the Age of Metternich", *Journal of Modern History*, XL (1968), 155-65. Rothenberg's reasons for the refusal of Carl's request (p. 157) completely ignore the personal and political enemity between Carl and Metternich.

[23] Kübeck, *Tagebücher*, I, 703.

[24] Erzherzog Carl, *Schriften*, VI, 327; Criste, *Erzherzog Carl*, III, 443f.

[25] Criste, *Erzherzog Carl*, III, 249f.

[26] Corti, *Metternich*, I, 293-305.

policy of military intervention against the revolution [27]. When the emperor ordered Metternich to brief the archduke on the political and military situation in order to change his mind, the chancellor provided no more information, in his own words, "than the archduke might have obtained from the *Allgemeine Zeitung*". In answer to Carl's criticism of his policy, Metternich expressed doubts about his courage and intelligence, and accused him of wanting to direct foreign policy [28].

There were other differences. Carl took a dim view of the chancellor's character and philosophy; he denounced his "self-seeking mediocrity" and opposition to the "spirit of time". In 1834 Carl said, "absolutism ... has outlived itself" [29]. In 1836 Metternich was to prevent, partly for political reasons, the marriage of Carl's daughter to the heir of King Louis Philippe which the archduke favored.

With this record of mutual detestation Carl's request to "the emperor" was not likely to be granted. But there were more objective reasons against putting him in charge of the war machine and the letter of refusal, signed by Ferdinand, stated them persuasively after fulsome praise for the archduke's qualities. The designation of a generalissimo would fit no permanent institution but would be tailored specially for him. It would thus be an extraordinary measure that might make an undesirable impression and be misinterpreted at home and abroad [30]. Kübeck called this a "clever" answer but pointed out that the real reason for the refusal was the certainty that the three regents would soon lose all influence and even their positions if Carl were to join the government with the entire military power in the hands of that popular hero [31].

The rejection of Archduke Carl was almost the last occasion on which the duumvires acted unanimously. During the next few months two issues increasingly divided them. Once again Kolowrat and Eichhoff insisted on reduction of the army estimates in order to reduce the growing deficit, and once again Metternich, supported by Clam and the president of the Hofkriegsrat, opposed it in view of the international situation and the increasing restlessness in Hungary. Metternich refused to withdraw the Austrian troops from the papal states because of Mazzini's activities; and with the question of Belgian independence still not solved, with the Carlist

[27] Criste, *Erzherzog Carl*, III, 441-44, 540-42.

[28] Kübeck, *Tagebücher*, I, 384-88.

[29] Erzherzog Carl, *Schriften*, VI, 534, 546; Friedjung, *Oesterreich 1848-60*, I, 3.

[30] Ferdinand to Carl, October 24, 1835, printed in Kübeck, *Tagebücher*, I, 707-09; Criste, *Erzherzog Carl*, III, 460-62.

[31] Kübeck, *Tagebücher*, I, 704.

civil war raging in Spain, with Switzerland near civil war over religious disputes, and with the imminence of the occupation of the Republic of Cracow – this was not a time to weaken the Austrian army. The dispute intensified to such a degree that Archduke Ludwig was forced to go to Metternich to effect a reconciliation with Kolowrat that did not, however, affect the underlying hatred. In the end, Kolowrat successfully resorted to his resignation gambit [32].

The second divisive issue was the question of readmitting the Jesuits, who had been tolerated in Galicia only [33], to the entire monarchy. Metternich saw the church as a political and social ally and as a bulwark against liberalism and revolution. "Church and state can be as little divided ... as the soul and the body", he wrote in 1851 [34].

Until about 1820 he had opposed the Jesuits but gradually began to favor them for political reasons while rejecting their religious views, in the same spirit in which he started to work for a concordat with Rome for the sake of his Italian policy and of church support for his struggle against the revolution [35]. In a memorandum of 1825, approving the admission of Jesuits to Galicia as a test case, he considered the problem from two standpoints, the "Austrian-administrative" one, and the "general juncture of time". Stressing what he saw as the Jesuits' chief purpose, the "conservation of church and throne, and victory of one and the other over its opponents", he clearly differentiated between this admirable aim of the "institution" on the one hand, and the excesses of "Jesuitism" on the other. For the first time he also questioned whether the Josephinian church policy really benefitted the state [36].

In the eighteen-twenties the Jesuits began a long and sustained campaign to be admitted to all provinces of Austria and to regain their old immunities of coming under the jurisdiction of emperor and general in Rome instead of local authorities and bishops. Emperor Franz, while favorably disposed towards them, postponed a decision in his usual manner. Under the new emperor the question became acute. Kolowrat had argued against any

[32] *Ibid.*, 719f. "I am determined to retire", Kolowrat told Kübeck. "He will remain at all cost", Kübeck noted in his diary (*ibid.*).

[33] Where they had fled after their expulsion from Russia in 1820.

[34] Srbik, *Metternich*, I, 306-13; *NP*, VIII, 556.

[35] Srbik, *Metternich*, I, 309f., 553; Fritz Valjavec, *Der Josephinismus* (2nd ed.; Vienna: Verlag für Geschichte, 1945), 89.

[36] *NP*, IV, 228-35.

concessions to the Jesuits from the beginning and continued to oppose them firmly [37].

But the pro-Jesuit party, led by Metternich and what Kübeck termed the "theological-diplomatic women's clique (*Weiberzunft*)" [38] – the empress, empress-mother, Sophie and, possibly, Metternich's own pious wife – claimed a victory in March 1836 when those Jesuits already in the empire were granted some of the privileges they had demanded, particularly in educational matters [39]. Josephinians, liberals and Kübeck deplored this as "a germ of dissolution and dissension" in the monarchy [40].

The dispute was by no means over. It continued to contribute to the accumulating tension and conflicts between the factions which were bound to lead to an explosion sooner or later. Ironically, the occasion for it, when it came, was provided not by a clash between the ministers but by Kolowrat's justified resentment of Archduke Ludwig's interference in his sphere.

[37] Ferdinand Maass, *Der Josephinismus* (Vienna: Herold, 1961), V, 91f., 20f.

[38] Kübeck, *Tagebücher*, I, 755.

[39] Maass, *Josephinismus*, V, 92f.

[40] Kübeck, *Tagebücher*, I, 721.

CHAPTER XIII

CREATION OF THE STAATSKONFERENZ

In the summer of 1836 Metternich returned to the subject of internal reform or the "organization of the *Centrum*" [1], as he liked to call it. It is clear from his correspondence with Clam that the unstable political and financial situation seemed to provide an opportunity to resolve personality and constitutional problems with one stroke. The two men discussed reform at length and agreed on all basic points.

Early in August Kolowrat wrote to Clam to warn him of polit4cal developments in Bohemia and the likelihood of "national bankruptcy" in view of the shrinking silver reserves. He also complained about his health and insisted on taking "a long vacation" which he defined as "removal from any contact with government business and petitioners" [2].

Clam forwarded the letter to Metternich with an interpretation of Kolowrat's demand for a vacation. The minister, he "understood", wanted to be largely relieved of his work and of the necessity to remain constantly in Vienna, but "wanted to be assured of the continuation of his influence". It would be difficult but not impossible, Clam thought, to find a formula for such an anomaly [3]. With an obvious reference to Kolowrat, he went on to warn Metternich that even complete agreement on the principles of internal reform was "no guarantee of complete consistency" in the application of those principles by the "principal persons". Clam also promised to send the chancellor an essay on reform [4].

Metternich replied that he had received a similar letter from Kolowrat and agreed that some arrangement for a "vacation" could be made. Kolow-

[1] "Centrum" was Metternich's favorite term for the central government, i.e. conference, Staatsrat and Hofstellen.

[2] Kolowrat to Clam, August 1, 1836, HHSA, Staatskanzlei, K.

[3] Kübeck ironically pointed out to Clam that "one anomaly more or less" would not change much in an anomalous government. (*Tagebücher*, I, 731).

[4] Clam to Metternich, August 8, 1836, HHSA, Staatskanzlei, K.

rat's warning of bankruptcy only proved that the finances could not be handled "capriciously". He regretted that Kolowrat "who acts only under the influence of his temper" could not understand that a "strong organization" was necessary in which everybody acted with "constancy and zeal" in his own sphere and cooperated in the Centrum. A confrontation with Kolowrat in Prague [5] could not be avoided but the chancellor was confident that it would all work out easily as long as it was done "quietly", since "right" was on one side and "emptiness" on the other [6].

With his next letter Clam enclosed the promised essay on reform [7]. Reorganization, he explained in his letter, was essential because of the "eccentric procedure of each institution"; the lack of a unifying structure was bad in itself and threatened to become a "public secret". The generally increasing bitterness about the activities of the Hofkammer and its president, Eichhoff, especially strong in the financial section of the Staatsrat which resented his influence on Kolowrat, illustrated the urgency of reform lest it come to a "formal rupture".

Clam also pointed out that the only subject on which he differed with Metternich was the latter's proposal to appoint the incumbent *Konferenz-Protokollführer* (keeper of the conference minutes), his secretary Hofrat Gervay, as Kabinettsdirektor. By combining these two important and confidential positions in the hands of a devoted follower, Metternich sought to reinforce his influence in the government and ensure greater control of the emperor. Clam objected that this transparent maneuver would make a bad impression on the public and enable jealous critics to denounce Gervay as a mere tool of the chancellor. It was, moreover, physically impossible to hold both offices, and not even necessary if Clam's reform plan was accepted.

The plan itself, obviously intended to persuade Archduke Ludwig rather than Metternich, was a model of lucid and logical presentation of ideas based mostly on Metternich's long held convictions. Like his mentor, Clam disavowed, for Ludwig's benefit, the necessity of "reform" – "a few wise and careful corrections" were all that was needed. His proposals addressed themselves to four "chief requirements". First the Staatsrat had to be returned to its proper function as the immediate adviser of the monarch in internal matters.

[5] In September, on the occasion of Ferdinand's coronation with the crown of St. Wenceslas.

[6] Metternich to Clam, August 11, 1836, *NP*, VI, 112f.

[7] Clam to Metternich, August 14, 1836, HSSA, Staatskanzlei, K.

Two faults had to be corrected: the Staatsrat's interference by executive action in the activities of the Hofstellen, and the withholding of certain business from its scrutiny. This was aimed at Kolowrat without mentioning him by name. Similarly, the urgent demand that "the political section must at last be given a really suitable head", managed to avoid naming Kolowrat, the incumbent, whom Clam obviously did not consider to be the "man of impartiality and firm principles" who was needed for this "eminent" position.

The second point of the plan concerned the conference. In order to turn it into "a true and permanent center for the deliberation of state affairs in the highest sphere", Clam proposed to replace its current chaotic and feeble practice by a well regulated procedure. It was indispensable to exclude all trivialities but none of the important questions (another dig at Kolowrat); to have regular sessions; and to admit Staatsräte and presidents of Hofstellen to the deliberations of subjects within their competence, thus removing the chief cause of their discontent and jealousy.

The relations among Staatsrat, conference and Hofstellen were Clam's third point. Misunderstandings, jealousies and jurisdictional disputes among them, he was confident, would be eliminated as a result of reforming Staatsrat and conference on the lines suggested.

His final point concerned the emperor's cabinet which, he hinted, had become vastly more important due to Ferdinand's disabilities. Its chief functions were the allocation of government business to the various institutions and the handling of petitions, a sensitive subject of "considerable influence on public opinion and private interests of innumerable people". Clam demanded the appointment of a more efficient, experienced and honest man than the incumbent, and the creation of a petitions committee to undertake a preliminary study of the 15 or 20,000 petitions a year Archduke Ludwig was now dealing with singlehandedly, and whose settlement, therefore, was now delayed by several months.

Clam's proposals had the double objective of eliminating Kolowrat's excessive power in the Staatsrat, and of rationalizing and modernizing the government. One could not be done without the other, but while the first aim was the immediate cause of the reform plan, the second was clearly not only of long range importance but based on ideas of long standing. In particular, Clam repeated Metternich's emphasis on division of functions and a strong and supreme ministerial conference, with a consequent reduction in the power of the Staatsrat. Although the chancellor's reaction to the essay is not recorded in the archives, there can be no doubt that he endorsed it wholeheartedly.

The anticipated confrontation of the two chief ministers at the Prague coronation did not resolve any of the disputed issues. A relatively minor matter, however, soon brought the unstable political situation to a climax. Some weeks earlier the Staatsrat had approved a reduction of import duties on sugar proposed by the Hofkammer. Alarmed sugar refiners and sugar-beet growing landowners appealed to Ludwig and persuaded the weak archduke to rescind the order. Kolowrat, already vacationing on his estate, subsequently agreed to the cancellation of the reduction but, deeply hurt and resentful of this interference in his domain, submitted to Ludwig a request for six months' leave of absence or for the acceptance of his "provisional resignation" [8].

The leave was granted but the resignation was not accepted. Ludwig obtained an order from the emperor to arrange, in conjunction with Metternich, for Kolowrat's duties to be discharged in his absence in order to avoid "a stoppage of business" [9]. Metternich described, in the letter he sent to Ficquelmont three months later, how he had recommended the leave, convinced that Kolowrat would return of his own accord "once the crisis was over". He had then asked the minister to tell him and the archduke how he wanted them to look after his functions during his absence, but Kolowrat – wrote Metternich – "unable to occupy himself with this subject", left it to his co-regents to settle everything [10].

With Kolowrat sulking on his estate, the way was now at last open for a major reform of the government. On September 30 Metternich drew up a long memorandum on the subject, addressed to Archduke Ludwig [11]. It was partly a recapitulation of his old ideas concerned with the proper functions of the institutions and the separation of government and administration, partly an analysis of governmental weaknesses. He stressed two chief defects. The first was the neglect to create a "center" which would bring all government business "to full maturity", ready for the final decision of the regent. Secondly, too many important documents obtained the emperor's signature through the "isolated *Referats-Weg*" (method of using special advisers) without ever going through normal channels.

This was already an indirect attack on Kolowrat, but Metternich did not hesitate to become explicit. Another defect, he pointed out, was the

[8] Kübeck, *Tagebücher*, I, 731; Bibl, *Zerfall*, II, 20f.; Fournier, "Kolowrat und Staatskonferenz", 270; Walter, *Zentralverwaltung*, 174.

[9] Ferdinand to Ludwig, September 16, 1836, HHSA, Praes., Kart. 4.

[10] Wertheimer, "Metternich und Staatskonferenz", 44, 51.

[11] Printed in Schlitter, *Vormärz*, IV, 92-97.

"regrettable relation" with Kolowrat who "carried a suffocating burden of work". The office of Prime Minister, "the *alter ego* of the monarch", he bluntly argued, was based on the weakness of a regent. No sensible servant of the state could want such a position, "impossible in our time and in our state". Austria's present "unprofitable" situation was a kind of "mixed" government in which neither one single man had the responsibility of decision nor did the heads of departments have any regular influence.

Hence, whether Kolowrat returned to the government or resigned, a reorganization was imperative but involved only "a more suitable utilization of existing norms rather than the creation of new ones". (Ludwig, like Emperor Franz, must not be frightened with the ghastly prospect of change). Hofstellen and Staatsrat had only to observe their old instructions from which they had lately departed. The *Staatskonferenz* [12], however, Metternich mildly urged, "needed a greater vivification and a better organized and regular procedure".

Unlike Clam who had virtually ignored Ludwig, Metternich thus subtly emphasized his position as principal regent and representative of the ruling family in the government. Compared with the chancellor's own past proposals and with Clam's recent incisive and succinct essay, this memorandum was a vague, rambling and indecisive effort. Clam, to whom Metternich had shown it, criticized it politely but firmly in an alarmed and exhortative letter [13]. While agreeing with the memorandum's principles, he found it "insufficiently *curative*" in view of the threatening danger, not so much of Kolowrat's "defection" but of the chaos produced by his ministerial procedures, and of the maneuvers of the "Eichhoffish liberal party". Kolowrat's party wanted him back and "*proclaimed his return*". Because of the general expectation of his early return, shared even by Archduke Ludwig, "something strong and public had *definitely* to be done and *without delay*".

"*Something must happen*", Clam pleaded, "*e i t h e r to exclude Kolowrat decisively, o r to tie his hands*" if he returned, and to replace his "*monopolizing arbitrary*" actions by proper procedures. It was correct of Metternich to propose a regularly meeting permanent conference, but a "modified continued vegetating" of the present totally insufficient structure was not enough, Clam warned. It must first be given more power and a regular

[12] This was the first time this term had been used for the conference. It foreshadowed its new structure and function.

[13] Clam to Metternich, September 28, 1836, HHSA, Staatskanzlei, P.M. All underlining in the original.

procedure, and its new "*organization*" had to be "*published* with intentional publicity", to make it creditable to the public and give its members self-confidence. It must be raised "to a higher intellectual purified region" rather than appear as just "*another* center" like the Staatsrat. This had to be done at once; there was no time for quiet "consolidation".

As a result Kolowrat and Eichhoff would be faced with the *fait accompli* of a "compact, organized" government armed with a "consistent procedure" which would put a stop to their arbitrary dictatorial "striving for omnipotence". Clam ended his urgent plea by assuring (but really exhorting) Metternich that "*he alone*", by "superiority of mind and will-power", was able to end the chaos of the government.

Metternich undoubtedly had the superior mind but his will-power lacked the ruthless determination essential to overcome the inertia of the archduke and the counterforce of hostile ministers. Taking note only of the sense of urgency but otherwise ignoring Clam's sensible advice and dire warning, he handed his memorandum, unchanged, to Ludwig on October 3. The archduke was convinced or at least impressed. He obtained Ferdinand's signature for a letter to Metternich that, expressing concern about the effects of Kolowrat's absence, ordered the chancellor to investigate the Staatsrat procedure in a "select (*enge*) conference" with the aid of heads of sections and other Staatsräte. As "chief of the Staatskonferenz" he was similarly charged to inquire into a reform of the conference. Clam who had drafted Emperor Ferdinand's letter explained to Metternich how he had skillfully interwoven the need for reform and the motive of Kolowrat's absence in order to establish a reason for the sudden reform activity and to preclude its abandonment in the event of the minister's return [14].

The Select Conference met on October 15 under the chairmanship of Ludwig, with Archduke Franz Karl, Metternich, the three heads of Staatsrat sections [15] and Hofrat Gervay participating. During the discussion of Staatsrat procedures there was general agreement that they had deviated considerably from the 1814 instructions and 1823 amendments. It was decided to have the extent and significance of the departures investigated by a committee under Metternich.

Four days later the Select Conference met again to hear the chancellor's report. This time five Staatsräte including Kübeck, attended as well. Metternich, according to Kübeck, was much more concerned with Kolowrat

[14] Kübeck, *Tagebücher*, I, 739f.; Clam's letter to Metternich (October 4, 1836) and his draft for Ferdinand's letter, printed in *OZV*, 267-69.

[15] Clam was one of them; the absent fourth was, of course, Kolowrat.

than with the Staatsrat. He explained that the minister's long leave of absence had created a gap in the government that had to be closed by a reorganization of the Staatsrat which had to be returned to its proper position. A committee of three Staatsräte was then charged with drafting new instructions for the Staatsrat. At a final meeting on October 20, after more debate and changes, the new rules were accepted and submitted for the emperor's signature [16].

Eichhoff, alarmed by these proceedings, sent a letter of protest to Metternich, demanding in strong terms that "all higher financial matters must be dealt with in the *Präsidialweg*" (through a presiding officer) as hitherto, that is, by a single responsible minister, as Emperor Franz had ordered. Owing to the necessity of acting according to a firm plan and often in secret, finances were "unsuitable for collective handling" in the Staatsrat. Eichhoff had enjoyed close personal relations with Kolowrat which had prevented any trouble with the Staatsrat over finances. No such relation was possible with another person. The finances would suffer accordingly, he warned Metternich, which was particularly unfortunate at this juncture when improvements promised early success. He also deplored the conflicts among sections and subsections certain to result from the removal of Kolowrat as "the central point of the Staatsrat" [17].

Metternich took no notice of this pressure. A few days later he submitted to the emperor – which meant to Archduke Ludwig – his report on the reorganization of the Staatskonferenz [18]. In a short historical survey he rejected Kaunitz's fusion of conference and Staatsrat as well as Emperor Franz's close contact of conference and Hofstellen. This led the chancellor to an analysis along familiar lines of the relations among governmental institutions and the monarch. The Staatsrat served as a "Gewissensrat", a "guardian" of the norm to the emperor who stood "on the tip of the pyramid". Controlling the executive actions of the Hofstellen, the Staatsrat was not a wheel in the clock-work but its pendulum. "Since even in the best regulated work friction was unavoidable", it was the "purely moral function" of the conference to act against these "disturbances which were the inevitable result of the hostile force".

Metternich did not define this vague force any further – he probably meant "the revolution" and its manifestations. He provided, however,

[16] Kübeck, *Tagebücher*, I, 732f.; Schlitter, *Vormärz*, IV, 97-100; Walter, *Zentralverwaltung*, 154. Schlitter and Walter wrongly date the second meeting October 28.

[17] Eichhoff to Metternich, October 20, 1836, HHSA, Praes., Kart. 4.

[18] Vortrag Metternich's, October 24, 1836, printed in *OZV*, 269-74.

a more concrete description of the Staatskonferenz's "most extensive purpose": It had neither to initiate business, as the Hofstellen did, nor to control other institutions, as the Staatsrat did; its activity only started where theirs left off. It was to "illuminate the most important" affairs of the state and to advise the monarch in the arbitration of disputes among the other bodies. Since the Hofstellen "stood before the monarch" and the Staatsrat "behind" him [19], the conference provided the natural juncture where all institutions could meet to defend their opinions; it thus effected "conciliation" and "enlightenment". Metternich also pointed out that the name "*Staats*-konferenz" indicated its sphere of activity which excluded all minor questions.

By the end of the month the work was completed. With unprecedented speed new instructions for both conference and Staatsrat were drawn up which included most of the points raised in Clam's essay. Those for the conference [20] had been drafted by Metternich and attached to his report. The ten points of the emperor's letter created the Staats-konferenz as an advisory body, without initiative or executive power, to handle particularly those "highest affairs of state" whose "measures and propositions" concerned "the whole of the state and of the government", or were significant deviations from the norm. It was to meet once a week and use "exclusively oral" procedure. Its permanent members – all active Staats- und Konferenz-ministers – were to be joined in relevant cases by the Staatsräte and presidents of Hofstellen concerned. Metternich was "confirmed" as "chief of the Staatskonferenz", in his absence the senior minister present was to preside.

The new instructions for the Sttatsrat [21], drawn up by the Select Conference, were based on those of 1814, modified by "the results of experience". The most important experience of the last two decades was Kolowrat's domination of the Staatsrat. By abusing his simultaneous positions as member of the conference and as head of the political section of the Staatsrat, he had become the virtual head of the entire Staatsrat. Hence the only two important changes in the regulations were designed to prevent this

[19] When Metternich read his report to a special conference, Kübeck was amused by, and contemptuous of, this "metaphorical language" which "we had to listen to with the seriousness of wise men". (*Tagebücher*, I, 734f.).

[20] Ferdinand to Metternich, October 31, 1836, printed in *OZV*, 275f. and Kübeck, *Tagebücher*, I, 744-46. It seems, however, that the letter was never signed, at least not until December. Signature was apparently held up while waiting for Kolowrat's agreement. (Wertheimer, "Metternich und Staatskonferenz", 45).

[21] Dated October 31, 1836, printed in *OZV*, 241-48.

in the future. Whereas in 1814 the membership had been defined as "Staats- und Konferenz Minister und Staatsräte", it was now to "consist of heads of sections and Staatsräte". Thus Kolowrat could either head a section without holding any other office, or, as a conference-minister, would be excluded from the Staatsrat. Another paragraph aimed even more clearly at the absent minister. "Nobody", it declared categorically, "hence also no head of a section" was authorized to remove any document from the regular procedure and to initiate a separate or "*praesidial*" transaction.

During the second half of October Kübeck was in an exceptionally censorious mood as far as Metternich was concerned [22]. He not only found fault with the chancellor's "flowery" and metaphorical language but also with the substance and object of his reform [23]. At the last meeting of the Select Conference Kübeck concluded that its actual purpose was to "exclude or paralyze" Kolowrat and that the aim to reorganize the government rationally in order to replace an incapacitated sovereign could never be realized [24]. Two months later he declared the true aim of the reforms to have been to pretend "to the ruling house and the nation" that the Staatsrat was an "imposing" institution, while using it, in reality, only for "preliminary work" and intending the conference, "and actually its head", to be the real "mainspring of government". Kolowrat was expected to object to these measures and resign [25].

There is much truth in Kübeck's observations. Undoubtedly Metternich continued to favor the conference at the expense of the Staatsrat as much for perfectly sound structural reasons as for the purpose of undermining Kolowrat's power base. It is also true that, under the circumstances, the reforms of October 1836, and particularly the new instructions for the Staatsrat, were primarily a move against Kolowrat. Yet it would be unjust to dismiss the reforms as being only an aspect of the decade old rivalry. They go back a quarter of a century and are in line with Metternich's previous proposals, modified to meet the changed situation.

[22] One hesitates to ascribe base human emotions to this exceptionally honest and fair man, but it must be recorded that he had just been promoted to *geheimer Rat* (privy councillor) and was to take the first opportunity, on November 19, to thank Kolowrat for his intercession (*Tagebücher*, I, 730, 732, 736).

[23] So much so that Srbik felt called upon to defend his hero by suggesting that Kübeck's "exaggerated grumbling" be ignored (*Metternich*, II, 572).

[24] Kübeck, *Tagebücher*, I, 733, 735.

[25] *Ibid.*, 741. Kübeck wrongly states that Kolowrat was invited to join the conference as minister or, *at the same time*, as head of section B. This would have been the exact opposite of Metternich's intention and violated the new Staatsrat instructions. Cf. chapter XIV, below.

Long before Kolowrat's advent, ever since 1811, the chancellor had stressed the importance of a conference composed of ministers charged with responsibility for executive departments. In 1821 he regarded a conference "the highest link in the ascending chain" of the governmental structure and deplored its virtual non-existence. Similarly, his insistence on a separation of powers, which was to become a crucial issue during the crisis of November 1836, long predated his rivalry with Kolowrat. As early as 1814 he had bluntly told the emperor that it was "impossible" to mix Staatsrat and conference without changing the former and paralyzing the latter. While this was ostensibly an attack on Wallis, it was, in fact, directed at Emperor Franz and his absolutist method of government that precluded any devolution of power to his ministers, all the more so since the weak Wallis was merely the emperor's mouth-piece.

The accession of Ferdinand had, however, changed the situation. There was no longer any point in giving advice to an emperor who could not understand it, much less benefit from it. The conference, therefore, in the absence of an official regent, assumed the function of a regency council, the highest authority in the state. It included the two men named as Ferdinand's chief advisers in his father's testament; Archduke Franz Karl; and, if he should so desire, Kolowrat. But in joining the Staatskonferenz the minister would have to give up his power in the Staatsrat, allowing that institution to assume its previous non-executive function of controlling the administration. On the other hand, if Kolowrat chose to remain at the head of section B, he would have to leave the conference and his influence would be correspondingly reduced.

In either case Metternich seemed at last to have reached his objective. The "Centrum" was reorganized on lines that would permit the government to act quickly and decisively; the influence and power of his rival was to be reduced to manageable proportions or eliminated altogether. No wonder, Princess Melanie in her diary called the "settlement" of the "conference affair" which had "painfully agitated" her husband, "an incalculable bliss" [26].

[26] *NP*, VI, 121.

CHAPTER XIV

THE CRISIS

Kolowrat had to be informed of the new developments. Clam was dispatched to Prague with the relevant papers and a letter from Archduke Ludwig [1]. At the same time Metternich undertook to elucidate the recent conferences and make their results palatable to the absent minister. In a conciliatory letter [2], with the calm confidence of a victor, the chancellor explained the necessity of making provisions to carry on the government in Kolowrat's absence. Speed had been essential in order to scotch rumors and lies circulating at home and abroad.

"Nothing new has happened", he assured Kolowrat as ingenuously as he had soothed Ludwig one month earlier. What existed already had merely been given new life. Two choices were now open to Kolowrat. He could remain senior section head or, if he preferred "more leisure and free movement", he could restrict himself to the position of an active minister. In either case he would "remain an active part of the Trinity", yet released from the pressing burden of work and able to enjoy several months' rest a year.

Although Kolowrat's susceptibility to flattery was well known, Metternich could not really have expected the minister to be so naive and gullible as to believe that nothing new had happened. No amount of praise for the "faithful and enlightened assistant" in the work of preserving the government, or apostrophe as a "friend ..., esteemed and honored" for many years, could disguise the fact that the "*mechanical regulation*" of the government had deprived Kolowrat of the greater part of his power.

[1] Clam to Metternich, November 2, 1836, HHSA, Staatskanzlei, K.

[2] Metternich to Kolowrat, November 1, 1836, HHSA, Staatsrat, Praes., Kart. 4; printed in Fournier, "Kolowrat und Staatskonferenz", 273-76. All underlining in all letters in this chapter are in the originals.

Illness, leave and resignation were instantly forgotten as Kolowrat decided not to throw up the game but to return to Vienna as soon as possible to confront his enemies.

Clam immediately warned Metternich to "proceed with great caution" because Kolowrat was likely to "yield to the momentary necessity with the arrière pensée of going his own way later". Hence Clam advised to negotiate "cautiously" and in writing about the minister's future position lest "everything once again be left to discretion", the abuse of which had caused all the present "confusion". Whatever Kolowrat's choice, he would have to be carefully watched since he would probably attempt to "work his way up again to the leading position in the Staatsrat" by "manipulation of documents" and influence over people [3].

A few days later, "at the moment of Count Kolowrat's arrival", Metternich sent a clear and succinct recapitulation of the situation and the necessary measures to Ludwig. He traced the defects of the government to two basic causes. One was the lack of a "clearly pronounced division and distribution of government business, the other, "the unsteady character of the *man charged with the bulk* of this business". Their combination led to uncertainties, intrigues and interruptions of government routines. Ludwig now had the opportunity, Metternich urged, to return the Staatsrat to its norm and to make the conference observe its new regulation.

Count Kolowrat must serve or retire from the service, for one cannot do both alternatively according to one's discretion. If he wants to serve, which I personally would prefer, then his position in the government must be regulated.

If he wanted to remain in the Staatsrat, Metternich stressed, he must head one of its sections because nobody could or must direct the entire institution. Nor must it contain a "*Ministerial Bureau*" [4] which implied a minister and changed the Staatsrat, in contradiction to its purpose, into an executive ministry. If, on the other hand, Kolowrat no longer wanted to work in the Staatsrat nor to confine himself to conference business, "*let him say what he wants*". He could not demand that things remain as they were because his irregular position had produced all the evil. Whatever he wanted, "he must condescend to *order*"; and Metternich appealed to Ludwig to elicit a clear formulation of Kolowrat's wishes and to insist that "order must be created" [5].

[3] Clam to Metternich, November 9, 1836, HHSA, Staatskanzlei, P.M.

[4] The more or less unofficial title of Kolowrat's office in the Staatsrat whose functions and scope had given him the virtual status of a Prime Minister.

[5] Metternich to Ludwig, November 13, 1836, HHSA, Staatskanzlei, P.M.

On November 14 Kolowrat returned to Vienna. During the next two days he had an audience with Ludwig in which he proposed to give up section B because of his health but demanded not to be confined to membership of the Staatskonferenz. He also saw Metternich twice to discuss the situation. Princess Melanie reported him to be in an understanding mood, approving recent measures and ready to content himself with becoming a conference member only. All seemed well but she confessed not to be full of confidence [6]. She was right to be wary.

When Clam drew up a report of the meetings which was supposed to express the consensus of the two men, Kolowrat demurred and insisted on adding his own comments. Metternich then arranged another meeting [7]. They had harsh words and the chancellor, as he told his wife, threatened Kolowrat with the use of his own tactics of resignation if the latter persisted in wrecking the government [8]. This passage in Princess Melanie's diary is the only mention of Metternich's resignation threat anywhere; he did not mean it seriously, if he ever made it.

In view of this failure to agree, both sides now put pressure on Ludwig to resolve the crisis in their favor. But the archduke's character was not equal to the situation. Despite his "weariness" of "this affair", Princess Melanie complained in her diary, "he does not have the strength to say: This must stop, I order it" [9].

Maintaining that "he felt his honor to be deeply hurt by the recent events", Kolowrat begged Ludwig to grant him another audience [10] before making any decisions [11]. Clam, on the same day, prepared draft letters for all contingencies, to be signed by the emperor. In his letter to Metternich [12] to which he attached the drafts, Clam also enclosed a "counter project" by Kolowrat in answer to the report on Metternich's position drawn up by Clam. The counter project has unfortunately been lost, but Clam described it as presenting no other difference to their views "than a question of vanity, dressed up as injured honor".

The most significant enclosure with Clam's letter was his draft for an official announcement in the *Wiener Zeitung*, also dated November 19.

[6] *NP*, VI, 123.

[7] Metternich to Kolowrat, November 18, 1836, HHSA, Praes., Kart. 4.

[8] *NP*, VI, 123.

[9] *NP*, VI, 124.

[10] Kolowrat seems to have had two audiences with the archduke, neither of which is recorded in the documents but only alluded to in their correspondence.

[11] Kolowrat to Ludwig, November 19, 1836, HHSA, Praes., Kart. 4.

[12] Clam to Metternich, November 19, 1836, HHSA, Staatskanzlei, P.M. with several enclosed draft letters in Clam's hand.

It proclaimed the formation of the Staatskonferenz but in very different terms to Emperor Ferdinand's letter of October 31. Where the latter had appointed Metternich as "chief of the Staatsconference", the announcement "placed" the conference "under the chairmanship of" the emperor. The usual provision for a replacement in case of absence or illness (which, in Ferdinand's case, would mean permanently) was omitted. Where the letter had deliberately neglected to name any members of the conference (not even Ludwig) but had merely defined them as all the "active ministers", the announcement named Archdukes Franz Karl and Ludwig, Metternich and Kolowrat as "permanent members". The active ministers were lumped together with Staatsräte, heads of Hofstellen and others as temporary members ("*Beisitzer*") in relevant cases. The same announcement also relieved Kolowrat, "at his own request", from the direction of section B.

Thus Metternich had already lost the leading position in the conference at a time when the crisis was at its height, with two weeks to go before its resolution. This is all the more puzzling in view of the apparently still fluid situation demonstrated by the inclusion, among Clam's enclosures of November 19, of a draft letter to be signed by Ferdinand "in case of Count Kolowrat's resignation". One is indeed tempted, as Walter conjectures [13], to attribute these changes to Kolowrat's pressure, all the more so since one of his marginal notes on Ferdinand's letter of October 31 had changed the instructions to read: "I reserve the presidency of the Staatskonferenz for myself. In my absence it will be taken over by my uncle, Archduke Ludwig ... or one of the members according to rank" [14]. Clam's draft would thus represent an important concession to Kolowrat. But even that victory, if it was one, did not satisfy the minister.

Three days later he renewed his efforts to convince Ludwig to return him to all offices and powers he had previously enjoyed. He sent the archduke copies of several letters and instructions addressed to him by Emperor Franz between 1826 and 1832, concerning his "position in the Staatsrat as well as in reference to the finances". Ludwig immediately passed them on to Metternich with the comment that he had seen all these letters when his brother had issued them [15].

[13] *Zentralverwaltung*, 187. Walter rightly stresses that Srbik, though aware of the announcement, did not recognize its importance. But Walter exaggerates the importance and correspondingly underestimates the role of Archduke Johann in resolving the crisis (*ibid.*, 191).

[14] Wertheimer, "Metternich und Staatskonferenz", 45.

[15] Kolowrat to Ludwig, November 22, 1836; Ludwig to Metternich, November 22, 1836, HHSA, Praes., Kart. 4.

Metternich drafted a reply, used almost verbatim by Ludwig, which accused Kolowrat of having usurped power in the past and of having similar ambitions for the future. "Despite thorough examination" of Franz's letters, Ludwig rightly maintained, they contained nothing about entrusting Kolowrat with "the *direction* of the Staatsrat" or "the *independent* management of *financial and internal* affairs", as Kolowrat had claimed. The various commissions had given him neither a permanent nor an independent position. It was impossible for a minister to remain in the Staatsrat if he did not head a section. That would "disturb the nature and purpose" of the Staatsrat and give the minister the appearance of heading the entire body. Kolowrat, Ludwig was certain, did not really want to become that, since it would invite "comparison with the reserved position of the monarch".

The real issue was, of course, Kolowrat's complaint that he "could never rank below Prince Metternich but demanded to be his equal". Ludwig remarked drily that "it cannot be altered that he has several years' seniority as minister", but he assured Kolowrat that as Staats- und Konferenzminister and permanent member of the conference he really was the chancellor's equal. Moreover, though this was a sufficiently important position, Ludwig was ready to allow him an additional sphere of action: all Staatsrat documents were to be submitted to Kolowrat's inspection, he was to be in charge of the personnel questions of the Staatsrat, and high finance as well as police matters "would be assigned to his domain", in accordance with his earlier discussion with Metternich [16].

Even this significant concession was not sufficient for Kolowrat. In his reply to the archduke [17], he defended himself against the accusation of being "an ambitious man striving for power". He had "*never* desired any advancement of my position or enlargement of my sphere of action". All he wanted was to return to his previous position which, however, seemed to have disappeared in all that reorganization under the guidance of Metternich. In a further appeal to Ludwig's aversion to change, he deplored the "constant changes and creation of hitherto unknown positions", that did not allow "the government to be carried on in the spirit of the late Emperor Franz".

[16] Ludwig to Kolowrat: Metternich's undated draft in HHSA, Staatskanzlei, P.M.; similarly worded draft, dated November 24, 1836 in HHSA, Praes. Kart. 4. The letter dated November 25, printed in Fournier, "Kolowrat und Staatskonferenz", 277-80, is identical with Metternich's draft.

[17] Kolowrat to Ludwig, November 26, 1836, HHSA, Praes., Kart. 4.

The public preferred the accustomed forms of government but, Kolowrat asserted, it was really less the form than the personalities in it that inspired trust or mistrust. After that allusion to Metternich's unpopularity, he admitted the irrelevance of the copies of Emperor Franz's letters he had sent to Ludwig; they were meant "only to prove that he enjoyed the honorable confidence of the emperor", he explained unconvincingly.

He agreed that all positions in the government must be clearly defined and expressed his "sincere wish that this definition would be strictly observed by *all*" – a patent reference to Metternich and the privileged position of foreign affairs. With false modesty he disavowed any ambition: he was "ready to devote his small ability to the state if it might prove useful, but equally ready to depart if his person no longer fitted the combination of the day". This was immediately modified – probably through fear of being taken at his word – by his offer to "submit to the continued direction" of the political section, because his request to be relieved of this position seemed to be "the only cause why I should not resume my position in the Staatsrat".

Kolowrat must have been perfectly aware that this wilful misreading of the situation violated the new regulations of the Staatsrat. Metternich, to whom Ludwig handed the letter, pointed out [18] that it was precisely Kolowrat's old position to which he now wished to return that had "produced the present deplorable situation". Kolowrat, the chancellor charged – thereby personifying one of his basic principles – mixed administration with government. "If he wants to *administer*, he must take charge of a Hofstelle; if he wants to *control*, let him accept the regulated position of a section head in the Staatsrat; if he desired to assume a high position in the *field of government*", Ludwig's offer of membership in the Staatskonferenz with the additional sphere of activity would give him that opportunity.

Kolowrat would have to choose between these three positions; they could not be fused. In two different passages Metternich attributed his rival's misunderstandings and "contradictions" to the influence of "others". Only Ludwig, he pleaded, could save the state from "this labyrinth", and he implored him to make a decision which only he could do without danger of being accused of self-serving motives. Such a decision would "concern not the individual but the basic principle" of government.

But Ludwig was too weak to pass firm judgment or take a decisive step. He contended himself with repeating Metternich's arguments in a letter

[18] Metternich to Ludwig, November 29, 1836, HHSA, Staatskanzlei, P.M.

to Kolowrat based on a draft drawn up by Clam and the chancellor [19]. He rejected Kolowrat's assertion that everything depended on personalities and not on forms. Since individuals were transient, institutions had to be regulated. Hence the chief task was to "consolidate" Staatsrat and conference "in the spirit of the late emperor" – Kolowrat's phrase – but also "with regards to current circumstances and needs". The revision of Staatsrat instructions had not altered a single organic clause of the 1814 rules.

Neither old nor new instructions allowed a central direction of the Staatsrat; hence to return Kolowrat to the head of section B would put him in a false position if he desired to have greater power than that of a section head, or, if he was satisfied with section B, would not give him enough scope. Ludwig here repeated Metternich's concise formulation:

A minister who is not a section head, does not belong *in* the Staatsrat; a minister who *is* section head, can function in the *Staatsrat* only in accordance with its instructions.

And again he offered Kolowrat a membership in the conference where "all important government measures" would be decided, with the concession of inspecting all Staatsrat documents which, as a section head, was impossible without breaking the rules.

It was important, Ludwig pointed out, to regularize Kolowrat's position in order to prevent a standstill of government business or rumors of his resignation each time he absented himself. The archduke ended by rebuking the minister for his remark about "combination of the day". There were instead, he stressed again, "circumstances and needs which demanded an orderly state of affairs".

This appeal to reason went unheeded. It ignored the one point of the controversy that was decisive for Kolowrat – Metternich's strong position in the conference and the consequent need for Kolowrat to balance this by his own strong position in the Staatsrat. Since his return to Vienna he had obtained two vital concessions: one was Metternich's demotion from chief of the conference to one of four members; the other, a large degree of control of the Staatsrat *in addition to* membership of the conference. The latter was a firm offer, made twice in writing by Ludwig. The significance of the former, however, is problematic, its very existence doubtful. The only evidence for it, before Metternich's letter to Ludwig of December 3,

[19] Ludwig to Kolowrat: undated draft in HHSA, Staatskanzlei, P.M.; similar draft, dated November 29, 1836, in HHSA, Praes., Kart. 4; similar letter, dated November 30, printed in Fournier, "Kolowrat und Staatskonferenz", 280-83.

1836 [20], is Clam's draft announcement of November 19. Whether that draft represented a concession to Kolowrat or whether he was even aware of it, are matters of speculation. Since the subject was never even alluded to in the correspondence between Ludwig, Metternich and Kolowrat, it can at most be assumed that Kolowrat did not consider this a binding concession. Hence his insistence on a stronger role in the Staatsrat than Ludwig's offer of the added sphere of activity seemed to provide.

A basic principle of the Staatsrat ever since its inception in 1760 had been the separation of administration and control, by not allowing any member of the Staatsrat to hold any other official position, especially not an administrative or executive one. Kaunitz had to defend this rule as early as 1762 [21]. Metternich, its strongest advocate in recent times, had permitted its violation in the case of Count Zichy, a personal friend and a man with no great ambitions [22]. With Kolowrat, however, the objectives of personal rivalry and political statecraft coincided to reinforce his conviction of the necessity of the separation of powers as part of the rational reorganization of the government as well as a move in the power struggle.

Hence all through November, during the acute stage of the crisis, the dominant note of Metternich's letters and drafts was the incessant stress on order, norms, rules and the precise definition of functions and spheres of activity. The Staatsrat must be returned to its norm, the rules for the Staatskonferenz must be observed, Kolowrat must "condescend to *order*" – these were his key phrases. But there was another, related, note as well: let Kolowrat say what he wants.

But that was exactly what Kolowrat would and could not do. Order was anathema to his character and nemesis to his power. Where Metternich was precise and stressed the future, Kolowrat was deliberately vague and evasive, and emphasized the past. His power and influence had, in the past, been based on a privileged position, in part conceded by Emperor Franz in violation of existing governmental norms. The new instructions and procedures of October 1836 had been tightly drawn to fence him in. He was now trying to break out, to resume his past informal vague position of power – "wrapped in an unhealthy fog" [23], as Metternich put it. Kolowrat, therefore, stressed personalities instead of forms, pretended the crisis

[20] See below, chapter XV.

[21] Hock-Bidermann, *Staatsrat*, 10, 20.

[22] See above, p. 33.

[23] In his letter to Ludwig of November 29, 1836.

to be a matter of his honor, and above all attempted to influence Ludwig and bring him to his side by playing on his horror of change.

Ludwig, unhappy with the entire situation and as unwilling as ever to make a decision, still backed Metternich at this stage – whether from conviction, personal sympathy or sheer indolence, it is hard to say. He passed all letters from Kolowrat to the chancellor and faithfully used drafts by Clam and Metternich for his answers.

Metternich's notes and drafts of this period show how preoccupied he was with the crisis and with the results of its possible solutions [24]. One note analyzed the "backlog of the secret cabinet". Another, entitled "regulations of the Centrum", stressed procedural matters concerning Kolowrat. One of its points demanded a new method of distributing subject matter ("hitherto Count Kolowrat was in charge of distributing Referate"); another emphasized the danger of Staatsräte reporting to the emperor alone, but "it is just as bad when Count Kolowrat or anyone else is the *exclusively permanent* witness attending the report". (Kübeck's reports were frequently attended by Kolowrat) [25]. An "agenda for the Staatskonferenz" included appointments of the highest officials, salaries for Staatsräte, creation of a conference bureau and a warning that Kolowrat's office must not be allowed a special place in the official ranking (*Staatsschematismus*).

The two most interesting drafts concerned the "chief principles of the Staatskonferenz and Staatsrat", and an elaborate argument against extensive powers for a single minister. The former, based on the reorganization of October, demonstrated the supreme position of the conference. With Metternich presiding (actually "the ranking" minister) but conceding to Ludwig the calling of meetings "at his discretion", its agenda covered new legislation, high finance (Eichhoff's and Kolowrat's domain), as well as subjects submitted by Ludwig or "any permanent member". Ludwig was clearly not meant to be a member of the conference.

The essay on the position of the monarch, subtitled "against ministerial government", examined the unique position of Austria as a multi-national empire, a bridge between north and south, occident and orient. The "key" to Austria's existence in this situation was the resistence of the parts (the provinces) to the "revolutionary fusion-system" called centralization. Hence the importance, as in no other state, of the monarch as the personal

[24] All undated, almost certainly written in November 1836, in HHSA, Staatskanzlei, P.M. and Praes., Kart. 4.

[25] Kübeck, *Tagebücher*, I, *passim*.

"central point of the government". A strongly organized government was more essential to the Austrian empire than any other, particularly in these times when "the entire social body was in feverish excitement and thrones were toppling daily". The personality of the monarch was thus of supreme importance, and when a third of the empire recognized constitutionally only the king as the source of executive and, partially, legislative power, "*ministers* did not fit this part". Constitutional monarchs – "le roi règne mais ne gouverne pas" – were quite unsuitable for Austria where the emperor had to exercise supreme power or, "if he could not, had to pretend to do it".

All aspects of the crisis were "extremely painful" for Metternich, he began to "look awful" and to find "distraction" only in the "affairs of the foreign ministry" [26]. But foreign affairs, too, began to reflect the crisis. *Le Courrier Français* of November 15 [27], for example, warned the French government not to "persist in seeking an alliance with Austria at the moment when" the only liberal minister seemed to have left the government which was now in the hands of the man who supported the Carlists in Spain. This doubtless did not alarm Metternich, but it underlined the urgency of resolving the crisis.

[26] *NP*, VI, 124 (Princess Melanie's diary).

[27] One of several foreign press cuttings of this period, collected for or by Metternich, in HHSA, Staatskanzlei, P.M.

CHAPTER XV

ARCHDUKE JOHANN'S INTERVENTION

As early as the first decade of the nineteenth century, the eight brothers of Emperor Franz formed a kind of party at court held together by a common desire for power. As we have seen, the imperial princes were, as a rule, jealously excluded by the emperor from real political influence. They were opposed by high officials, both military and civilian, and by the favorites of Franz [1].

During the thirties, the Sardinian envoy described them as being restless at being kept out of state affairs and keen to replace government by ministers with government by archdukes [2]. The French ambassador recalled how the archdukes waited upon Metternich in his antechamber, ranged against the wall, hat in hand, "like a corporal before his captain" [3]. While this probably referred to the lesser princes of the Italian line and certainly not to senior archdukes like Carl or Johann, it was symptomatic of Metternich's contempt for most of them. It is hardly surprising, therefore, that Kübeck noted that "all" the archdukes favored Kolowrat [4].

Actually, Metternich had an agreeable relationship with Archduke Rainer, Ludwig's older brother. As viceroy of Lombardy-Venetia, Rainer demanded some real power and authority, and less dependence on Vienna. In this he was frustrated by Emperor Franz rather than by Metternich who largely supported his justified claims [5]. It was with the three older brothers that the chancellor was on bad terms. Since these three, Carl, Joseph and Johann [6], were very close to each other and regarded themselves as the

[1] Krones, *Geschichte Oesterreichs 1792-1816*, 53-56.

[2] Sambuy, *La Politica Estera*, I, 189; Sybel, "Staatskonferenz", 360.

[3] Sainte-Aulaire, *Souvenirs*, 110.

[4] Kübeck, *Tagebücher*, I, 757.

[5] Haas, *Metternich and Reorganization*, 140f., 143-45.

[6] The oldest, Ferdinand III, Grand Duke of Toscana, took no interest in Austrian politics and died in 1824.

guardians of the dynasty, the sum of their strained relations with Metternich outweighed in significance their individual attitudes.

The chancellor's lifelong enmity with Carl has already been examined [7]. In a similar manner, Metternich's interference in the private affairs of Joseph, palatine of Hungary, exacerbated political antagonism. During the Napoleonic period the archduke was a strong opponent of Metternich's foreign and Hungarian policies. In 1812 the latter intercepted correspondence between Joseph and his sister-in-law, Empress Maria Ludovica. The letters were critical of the pro-French foreign policy of Emperor Franz and his Foreign Minister; they contained mutual assurances of friendship and some complaints by the empress about her husband's bad moods. Showing the letters to the emperor with some absurd hints of an illicit love affair, Metternich tried to obtain a prohibition of further correspondence. Although, apparently, unsuccessful in this, the episode can hardly have endeared him to the palatine [8].

From the same period and from similar political conflicts derived Johann's hostility. Early in 1813 he called for immediate war against Napoleon, with his brother Carl as head of the army. When he was successfully opposed by Metternich, he complained that the Foreign Minister "wants everything and does not understand it; hence he interferes everywhere and Schwarzenberg obtains the command through him" [9]. One month later Johann's "Alpenbund" plot [10] to organize a rising against Napoleon in the alpine provinces was discovered and frustrated by Metternich.

From then on Johann was completely shut out from political influence, as Carl had been since Wagram. He felt bitter about it and was aware that he was feared as much for his honesty as for his ability [11]. After Franz's death the triumvirate had even more urgent reasons than the late emperor to exclude the two ablest archdukes, and only once allowed them a public role when they were paraded before the Tsar at Teplitz.

Johann always held Metternich responsible for keeping him from high office, especially in his beloved alpine lands [12]. But unlike Carl, who thought

[7] See above, pp. 78-79.

[8] Bibl, *Kaiser Franz*, 204-08; Corti, *Metternich*, I, 349-56.

[9] Erzherzog Johann, Tagebücher, January 19-26, 1813.

[10] Johann defined its aim as "freedom and constitution suitable to the circumstances of the country, suppression of everything oppressive, struggle against superiority and arrogance, cooperation to expedite a lasting peace". (*Ibid.*, February, 24-27, 1813). Metternich could have identified only with the last of these objectives.

[11] *Ibid.*, December 27, 1817.

[12] *Ibid.*, January 8, 1836.

it "beneath his dignity to be on good terms with" Metternich, as Johann put it, the latter felt it to be his duty to serve his emperor by trying to cultivate friendly relations with his ministers, with Metternich as he had with Counts Ludwig Cobenzl and Philipp Stadion, both former Foreign Ministers [13]. By 1817 he had changed his mind about Metternich's easy-going idleness and now agreed that he was "called upon by ability, intelligence and experience ... to guide the helm of the state" [14].

There were still political differences similar to Carl's. A moderate liberal like Kübeck, Johann shared the latter's dislike of labels which, at best, were useless, at worst, a weapon to destroy good men [15]. Hofkanzler Pillersdorf, Kübeck and others, Johann complained, were called "liberals, a platitude by which one covered a lot without quite knowing what one meant". He was not "interested in such terms, only in ability, disposition and performance". He admitted to be a liberal if that meant "to oppose all stagnation and wishes to return to the old, rusty, no longer suitable" [16].

An example of this was the problem of the Jesuits. Johann found it "strange that the wise and intelligent Metternich favored them", believing to find in them a support for monarchic principles, but forgetting "what history teaches us", that they support these principles or anything else only as long as they serve their purposes. Friendly or hostile, their means were unscrupulous – "may God preserve us from such institutions!" [17].

Added to these personal and political disputes was Johann's loyalty to his brother Carl whom he called his "best friend" [18]. He took Carl's side in the questions of the Orleans marriage and of the army command in 1835. As late as January 1837 he still regretted his brother's failure because he was convinced he had the complete confidence of the army and was alone competent to lead it. But Johann would have preferred a gradual approach after first reconciling Carl and Metternich as the surer way to success [19].

With all these factors predisposing Johann to hostility towards Metternich, it was quite natural that he found Kolowrat more agreeable. In 1832

[13] *Ibid.*, December 27, 1817.

[14] *Ibid.*, December 31, 1817.

[15] Kübeck thought knowledge, talent and honesty more important than the "party weapon of names". To be designated a liberal would deprive a man of his position despite long and loyal service to the state. (*Tagebücher*, I, 587f. Cf. *ibid.*, 772).

[16] Erzherzog Johann, Tagebücher, January 9, 1836.

[17] *Ibid.*, January 14, 1836.

[18] Sutter, "Erzherzog Johanns Kritik", 190.

[19] *Ibid.*, 180.

he called him "an excellent, noble man, the most faithful friend of the emperor ... to meet him is the greatest pleasure for me" [20]. Exactly four years later he still found him "noble, honest, open" [21]. Perhaps Kolowrat's talk about having tried to create for Johann a similar position in the alpine provinces to Rainer's in northern Italy but having been prevented by Metternich [22] may have contributed to the archduke's favorable opinion of the minister.

Worried about the cabinet crisis, reacting to wild rumors of government changes and finally following an urgent plea by Kolowrat, Johann arrived in Vienna at the end of November [23]. Kolowrat had already approached him at the coronation in Prague, just before the crisis broke, to warn him of the imminent bankruptcy due to Metternich's inexperience with finances and extravagant spending on Carlists and other foreign policy adventures. Johann had encouraged him then to continue his struggle with the chancellor and to see to it that the archdukes were consulted [24].

Now, in Vienna, Johann's good impression of Kolowrat was only slightly modified. During a busy round of consultations and conferences with Ludwig, Metternich, Clam and Kolowrat, with Franz Karl, Sophie and the empress-mother as well as with other high officials, Johann – not for the first time – heard praise of Kolowrat's popularity and financial honesty balanced by serious complaints about his usurpation of government business, destruction of Staatsrat and other routines, arbitrariness of his officials, and periodic absenteeism. Johann either attributed these attacks to the "Rothschild Jewish party" against whom Kolowrat had preserved his independence, or he found excuses for the minister's failings in his irritability caused by his affliction [25].

Johann saw the root of the evil and the cause of the crisis in what he termed "ministerial government", the direction of the state by Metternich, to the exclusion of the archdukes. "We do not want a *majordomus*!" he told

[20] Erzherzog Johann, Tagebücher, January 14, 1832.

[21] *Ibid.*, January 14, 1836.

[22] Srbik, *Metternich*, II, 15.

[23] Unfortunately some of Johann's diaries were destroyed during World War II, including those dating from summer 1836 until January 1837. The crucial period of Johann's intervention in the crisis cannot, therefore, be documented from his diaries. Srbik, who still had access to them, used them extensively in his account (*Metternich*, II, 14-18) to which reference will be made in the following pages.

[24] Srbik, *Metternich*, II, 15.

[25] *Ibid.*

his brother Ludwig [26] and, demanding that one of the archdukes should preside over the Staatskonferenz, tried to talk him into that position or at least to take some decisive step. But Ludwig refused, insisting evasively that he had to work in the background, "invisibly", to keep the government going [27].

The climax of Johann's series of conferences was his crucial discussion with Metternich, lasting for three and one half hours [28]. He accused the chancellor bluntly of wishing to "bring about a Merovingian era and be like Pepin", and charged him with the "fearful blunder (*Mordsschnitzer*) of wanting, as it were, to become president". Metternich almost lost his temper but quickly calmed down and pointed to Kolowrat's "unorganic and irregular position and attitude". Johann agreed that "his good Kolowrat" had indeed laid himself open to attack but only in order to speed up government business. Metternich then conceded without trouble the archduke's chief demands: one of the princes had to preside over the Staatskonferenz though the emperor would be its nominal head; Ludwig, Franz Karl and Metternich were to be permanent members; Kolowrat was to choose between returning to the Staatsrat as section head or join the Staatskonferenz with control of financial and internal matters [29].

This agreement thus confirmed the two concessions Kolowrat had already obtained – one firmly, one doubtfully – during the negotiations in November. First, Metternich lost the presidency of the conference. Secondly, Kolowrat retained a significant degree of control over the Staatsrat, and a strong and potentially decisive voice in internal and financial policies. On the other hand, his position was now to be regularized and his sphere of action clearly delimited. Superficially, at least, Metternich's concept of the division of powers had prevailed and Kolowrat was excluded from the Staatsrat. (Nobody expected him to choose to remain head of section B and spurn the conference). In view of past experience, however, and of Kolowrat's character, as well as of his newly created special position vis-à-vis the Staatsrat all of whose work he was now authorized to inspect, the prospect for a continued separation of powers and for a limitation of Kolowrat's influence was gloomy.

Johann continued his consultations more determined than ever to "erect a wall against the presumptions of ministers and to honor the archdukes".

[26] Bibl, *Dämon*, 307.

[27] Srbik, *Metternich*, II, 574, note to p. 16.

[28] Kübeck deplored the undignified role of archdukes as mediators between "two oligarchic ministers". (*Tagebücher*, I, 739).

[29] Srbik, *Metternich*, II, 16.

He encouraged Ludwig to remain firm and considered it his final duty to persuade "the noble Kolowrat" to accept the settlement and not to "cling to" semantics [30].

Metternich, too, felt it was necessary to strengthen Ludwig, not so much in order to honor the archdukes but to keep Kolowrat in check. In a final letter [31] he implored the archduke to "fill the gap" opened by Emperor Franz's death. The "true cause of the inexcusable evil" was the fact that the government "was still following the same track as under the late monarch". Then, despite delays and other defects, "*there was an emperor*", able to say "*I will* or *I will not*". This power of decision was now missing. "Your excellency must seize the *I will* or *I will not*", Metternich pleaded.

He frankly admitted that this was indispensable as a means of controlling Kolowrat. The latter, "*in a healthy condition*", tended to take on only such business as he found "agreeable", while pretending to guide and decide everything. "*During his periodic illnesses*" his share of the work must be absorbed by a "pedantic regulation" of government routine. Ludwig would have to insist on a "regulated distribution" of business to the Staatsrat, the Staatskonferenz, and to Kolowrat himself. The minister, like the Staatsrat, would have to submit to a second deliberation by the conference of important subjects under his control. It was up to Ludwig to decide what was important.

On the question of the presidency of the conference, Metternich thought it advisable that the emperor should preside "sevei al times a year in person". (This was probably intended as a tactical move to hide the existence of a *de facto* regency). Normally, however, this function should be exercised by Ludwig, and in his absence by the ranking minister but never by Archduke Franz Karl, in order to avoid putting him into a false position. As heir-apparent he should keep himself informed but should never actively participate in the government.

According to Johann's diary [32], Ludwig was somewhat annoyed with this letter, complaining that everything was polemical with Metternich and expressing reluctance to tie Franz Karl's hands. He promised, however, to consider all of the chancellor's points. Two days later, at the decisive conference of December 5, it was clear that Ludwig essentially accepted Metternich's ideas despite his reservations and reluctance to take a firm lead. Only four persons attended the conference, Ludwig, Metternich,

[30] Johann's diaries, quoted in Srbik, *Metternich*, II, 17.

[31] Metternich to Ludwig, December 3, 1836, HHSA, Staatskanzlei, P.M.

[32] Srbik, *Metternich*, II, 17.

Franz Karl and Kolowrat. The first two were in basic accord and no trouble was expected from the heir-apparent. Hence the only purpose of the meeting was to obtain Kolowrat's final agreement to the settlement negotiated by Johann with all parties.

Ludwig started the proceedings by reading a memorandum that summed up the settlement [33]. Pointing out that the "unpleasant situation which the public calls a ministerial crisis" had to be ended, he demanded cooperation and unity in the highest sphere of government on the basis of the instructions for Staatskonferenz and Staatsrat issued on October 31 [34]. These would provide the government with the "qualities of order, firmness and unity". In order, however, to present the conference to the world as the "source of highest authority in the state", Ludwig proposed to change its "outward appearance". The emperor himself was to preside over it; Franz Karl, Ludwig, Metternich and Kolowrat were to be its permanent members, with ministers, section heads, Staatsräte and presidents of Hofstellen as temporary members for relevant subjects.

Turning to Kolowrat, Ludwig asked him directly to clarify his position which should be "influential, important but regulated, and calculated to enable him to rest periodically" without disrupting government business or giving rise to new rumors. But it had to be based on the "irrefutable proposition" about the incompatibility of section head and active minister which Ludwig repeated verbatim from his letter of November 29.

When Ludwig had finished, the meeting accepted his proposed change of the conference as well as an amendment offered by Franz Karl to have Ludwig preside over the conference in Ferdinand's absence. Kolowrat then asked, before answering Ludwig, in what form he would be able to direct those departments of the Hofkammer which were not subject to Staatsrat control. Obtaining the assurance that he would be able to use members of the financial section of the Staatsrat to deal with these subjects, Kolowrat agreed to give up his position as head of section B and take up that of an "active Staats- and Conferenzminister" in the conference with the additional sphere of activity indicated by Ludwig [35].

All that remained was for Ludwig to go through the farcical motion of reporting to the emperor and to enclose, for his signature, letters giving

[33] Ludwig's memorandum, December 5, 1836, printed in *OZV*, 279-81.

[34] See above, p. 89, footnote 20.

[35] Protokoll of conference of December 5, 1836, written by Metternich and signed by those present, printed in *OZV*, 277-78.

effect to the new organization [36]. Emperor Ferdinand signed everything without understanding a word or evincing the slightest interest. The "Bureau" of the conference (a kind of chancellery) and its department handling personnel matters were entrusted to Metternich who had asked for this in his letter to Ludwig of December 3, in order to prevent their being seized by "intrigue" – a euphemism for Kolowrat. The latter was authorized to see all Staatsrat documents and to bring important subjects directly to the emperor's notice or send them to the conference. He was charged with all personnel matters of the Staatsrat and with directing high finance and credit operations as well as police matters. In connection with the last item, Kolowrat was instructed to keep Metternich informed of all reports on public opinion and anything touching upon foreign policy [37].

The crisis was over. How did the participants evaluate its results? Archduke Johann thanked God that he had succeeded in creating a "sharp division" between Metternich's direction of foreign affairs and Kolowrat's of interior and financial matters. Neither would interfere in the sphere of the other; Ludwig alone would be informed of everything and alone would hold the power in his hand [38]. Johann was satisfied and, as Kübeck put it, "proclaims to everyone the laurels he had won on this occasion". He was content to remain outside the government and play the role of an unbiased observer reporting public opinion to the rulers [39].

Kolowrat informed Kübeck that Johann had told him "with pleasure" how he had duped Metternich and cheated him out of his power by persuading Ludwig to take his office as chief of the Staatskonferenz seriously, to exercise it himself and not leave it to the chancellor [40]. Whether or not Johann had actually said this, it can safely be taken as Kolowrat's own view of the situation. He evidently felt very confident of influencing Ludwig in his favor.

Metternich's camp was reasonably content with the result of the government reorganization. Count Heinrich Bombelles, tutor of Archduke Franz, the son of Franz Karl and Sophie, and the future Emperor Franz Josef,

[36] Vortrag Ludwig's, letters from Ferdinand to Ludwig, Kolowrat, Nadasdy, Hofstellenpräsidenten, December 12, 1836, HHSA, Praes., Kart. 4; all except letter to Nadasdy printed in *OZV*, 281-85.

[37] In the original undated draft for Ferdinand's letter to Kolowrat, it was "left to [Kolowrat's] discretion" to inform Metternich of public opinion reports and whatever else he might deem useful. (HHSA, Praes., Kart. 4).

[38] Srbik, *Metternich*, II, 19.

[39] Kübeck, *Tagebücher*, I, 742, 761.

[40] *Ibid.*, 750.

who was on intimate terms with Metternich and his close ally, saw the decision of December 5 as a modified victory for the chancellor [41].

Metternich himself was, or pretended to be even more pleased. Although he had lost the predominant role in the government that the instructions of October 31 had given him, he found consolation in the fact that Kolowrat's position was now clearly defined and limited, and that by resigning from the political section of the Staatsrat his domination of that body was rendered much more difficult. Metternich never admitted, to others and probably even to himself, that his rival might have derived greater benefit from the reorganization than he did.

"The work that has just been completed is of great significance; it puts people and things into a correct, clear and exact light", Metternich assured the Austrian ambassador in St. Petersburg, in a long letter written "for the personal information" of the Tsar to whom it was to be shown [42]. Referring to the Staatskonferenz, the chancellor declared that "what had the value of a dream for me for twenty-eight years, now assumes at last a living form". The letter was meant as a reassuring account of recent events, to disperse the doubts and fears Tsar Nicholas had expressed at Teplitz about Austria's internal weakness. It gives the impression of Metternich dispelling his own apprehensions as much as those of the Russian emperor.

Kübeck, as usual, displayed the most acute political judgment.

> Archduke Johann, presumably assisted by Ludwig and a part of the imperial family, effected a compromise that is little different from a complete defeat of Prince Metternich. ... In effect [Kolowrat] is supreme head of the Staatsrat, master of the money power, of all employment and of the fate of all officials (through the police), head of the entire camarilla and – through his position – the deciding spokesman in the conference [43].

Kolowrat had thus regained the greater part of the influence and power he had wielded before the crisis, with the additional advantage of being officially confirmed in much of what had previously been vague, undefined and even contrary to regulations. He now essentially fulfilled the functions of a Prime Minister, an office regarded by his rival as "quite impossible" for Austria and suitable for "no sensible servant of the state".

[41] Wertheimer, "Metternich und Staatskonferenz", 45. Bombelles is the "Austrian statesman" (*ibid.*, 41) to whose diary Wertheimer had access. See Srbik, *Metternich*, II, 571, note 1 to p. 2.

[42] Metternich to Ficquelmont, December 14, 1836, printed in Wertheimer, "Metternich und Staatskonferenz", 48-54.

[43] Kübeck, *Tagebücher*, I, 742.

CHAPTER XVI

DREIGREISENREGIMENT

Whoever was the real beneficiary of the crisis, it was not the Austrian state. It was soon obvious that nothing had changed, that, in the words of Metternich's contemporaries, "the state machine was panting along in the old track, guided by no one, checked by no power, driven by nothing but itself according to the law of inertia" [1].

If Metternich seriously believed that his twenty-eight year old dream had come true in a conference consisting of two incompatible rivals and an indecisive arbiter, he must soon have been bitterly disappointed. The assignment of business to the Staatskonferenz was far from systematic – "rhapsodical", Hartig called it – more often based on subjective than objective criteria. Ludwig soon reintroduced written procedure instead of discussion and exchange of ideas [2], probably as much from weariness with the chronic squabbles of the rival ministers as from personal inclination.

In the Staatsrat, Kübeck complained, the four sections worked in isolation. Kolowrat was "outside the Staatsrat and yet ... above it as an independent power", always "led by a string but forever in the delusion of independence". The whole government was to Kübeck a "symbol of disorganization", a "*monstrum horrendum*" that was the work of Metternich and the other rulers who, having "grown grey in intrigue" and being used to deception and falsehood, had difficulty in "creating an orderly organism" [3].

Above all, Ludwig was incapapble of becoming "the soul of ... the Staatskonferenz", as Clam demanded [4]. Kübeck blamed him for doing no more than imitating Emperor Franz in playing off one rival against the

[1] Schmidt, *Zeitgenössige Geschichte*, 524.
[2] Hartig, *Genesis*, 37.
[3] Kübeck, *Tagebücher*, I, 755.
[4] Srbik, *Metternich*, II, 21.

other by never allowing one to gain a complete victory over the other and by not completing important measures advocated by either. Hence the government "creeps along, more busy than efficacious" [5].

In accordance with Archduke Johann's intentions, Metternich was excluded from all internal and financial affairs. When he complained that no documents were sent to him on these subjects, Kolowrat coldly answered that Ludwig and no longer Metternich was president of the conference, that all documents went to the archduke, and that it was up to Ludwig to send them to the Staatskonferenz or to withhold them. The archduke, who had already told Johann that he would work on these subjects with Kolowrat alone ("The others do not need to know everything"), approved of Kolowrat's attitude and both, in turn, were encouraged by Johann [6].

Along with governmental chaos political factiousness had survived the crisis and thrived as never before. Every new appointee to an important position was closely examined as to his support for either Metternich or Kolowrat, and was ardently wooed by both factions. A neutral attitude became almost impossible [7]. To Kübeck, this was government "not according to principles but according to interests". The motto of this "enfeebled despotism" was "preserve the bad and the good as it is; just make no changes!". This, he warned, was the road to revolutionary anarchism and the government was well on the way there [8]. To the people at large the subtle distinctions of political factions meant nothing. Metternich's "trinity" was popularly known as the "*Dreigreisenregiment*" (government by three old men) [9].

By February 1837 the political situation had deteriorated to such an extent that Bombelles noted in his diary: "New ministerial crisis. Intrigues by Kolowrat in order to destroy the conference". Kübeck forecast an imminent "catastrophe" [10]. The immediate cause seems to have been a plan by Kolowrat to reorganize the government. He wanted to abolish the conference and the sectional division of the Staatsrat whose work was to be dealt with by eight Staatsräte among whom all business would be distributed and who would unite to form a council [11]. This arrangement

[5] Kübeck, *Tagebücher*, I, 767.

[6] Srbik, *Metternich*, II, 21, largely based on Johann's diaries.

[7] Wertheimer, "Metternich und Staatskonferenz", 119; Kübeck, *Tagebücher*, I, 760f.

[8] Kübeck, *Tagebücher*, I, 751f.

[9] Victor Bibl, *Metternich in neuer Beleuchtung* (Vienna: Seidl, 1928), 65. In 1837 Metternich was 64, Kolowrat 59, and Ludwig 53 years old. Ludwig's "phlegmatic and sleepy" appearance (Sainte Aulaire, *Souvenirs*, 339) probably made him look much older.

[10] Wertheimer, "Metternich und Staatskonferenz", 112; Kübeck, *Tagebücher*, I, 755.

[11] Wertheimer, "Metternich und Staatskonferenz", 112.

would abviously greatly facilitate Kolowrat's domination of the entire body.

This plan, according to Bombelles, was part of a plot to get rid of Metternich, Clam and two Staatsräte (including Kübeck) who were "allied" with them. When Ludwig refused to cooperate, Kolowrat attempted in vain to engage the aid of Franz Karl by enticing the archduke with promises of making him instead of Ludwig the emperor's deputy. "It seems", wrote Bombelles, "that Archduke Johann was behind this (*derrière le rideau*)", believing that Franz Karl could easily be persuaded to accept a "government of uncles" that would at last provide the influential positions he had long felt due to himself and his brother Carl. Franz Karl's loyalty to Ludwig and Metternich, however, frustrated this plan, at least for the time being [12].

During the last few months since the great crisis, Metternich had tried to gain Kübeck's support and had increasingly taken him into his confidence [13]. But Kübeck was more impressed with Clam who also began to share his plans, ideas and criticisms [14]. He greatly respected the general whom he called "ambitious ... with noble aspirations, righteous, a man of talent, rare culture, decisive chaıacter and purposeful activity" [15]. This was high praise indeed by a man as skeptical and exacting as Kübeck. Not surprisingly, he considered Clam to be "the best and clearest head, the purest man among the members of the government" [16], and largely came to share his views of the political situation.

Kübeck's identification with the Metternich faction was made easier by his growing disgust at the lies and intrigues by Kolowrat and Eichhoff. Once, when he challenged the former's prediction of imminent bankruptcy by pointing out that Eichhoff had described the financial situation to the government only a few months ago as so brilliant that hardly any other state in Europe could equal it, Kolowrat laughed and said, "yes, that was a lark by Eichhoff which he now regrets. We are all human. He had some requests then" [17].

Clam was deeply worried about the weakness of the government and the excessive power of Kolowrat, annoyed by the latter's refusal to grant his financial demands for the army, and aware of Metternich's irresolution and

[12] *Ibid.*, 112f.
[13] Kübeck, *Tagebücher*, I, 761f., 784.
[14] *Ibid.*, 761, 774f., 777, 781.
[15] *Ibid.*, 768.
[16] *Ibid.*, 761.
[17] *Ibid.*, 759, 786.

weakness [18]. As a result of the February crisis he began a campaign against Kolowrat that he was to continue intermittently until his death in 1840. The first shot of his offensive was a passionate call to action addressed to the chancellor [19].

He began by reminding Metternich that he had promised to "complete and enliven" the measures taken after the November crisis. But nothing was done while the opponents continued their evil work. Reform and strengthening of the government were urgently required, particularly a reorganization of section B and of conference procedure. As long as nothing was done, much of Kolowrat's strictures was justified. His intentions, however, were "impure", for he wanted to destroy, not to improve, what he censured with the aim of achieving unlimited rule in internal affairs. Ludwig was opposed to changing the institutions but his feelings towards them were at best "lukewarm". He was inclined to neglect them in favor of an "administrative cabinet government" that would open the way to Kolowrat's predominant influence.

From these premises Clam concluded that three courses were possible: to do nothing, to ask Kolowrat for his own reform ideas, or "to forestall Kolowrat and neutralize his plan" by inviting him to participate in the reforms. Since they were "dealing with a weak but cunning enemy" who "shied at the light and at open feud", and since Ludwig was incapable of exercising decisive will-power, Clam urged Metternich to take up the work of reform.

It was in vain; Metternich could not be moved to action.

It was Kolowrat who took the initiative again during the summer. Taking advantage of the absence of the chancellor who was taking the waters at Teplitz, he renewed his attempt to persuade the court, vacationing in Ischl, to agree to his scheme of destroying the conference and reforming the Staatsrat [20]. But Clam was present in Ischl, too, and able to warn Metternich.

He reported to him [21] that Kolowrat in a recent frank "outpouring (épanchement)" had clearly stated his hostility for the conference and his intention to "neutralize" it. When Clam had protested that all it needed was a reform of its procedure, Kolowrat had countered that Ludwig hated

[18] *Ibid.*, 758, 770, 774f.; Srbik, *Metternich*, II, 22; Wertheimer, "Metternich and Staatskonferenz", 113.

[19] Clam to Metternich, March 18, 1837, HHSA, Staatskanzlei, P.M.

[20] Wertheimer, "Metternich und Staatskonferenz", 113.

[21] Clam to Metternich, July 17, 1837, HHSA, Staatskanzlei, K.

the conference and that Franz Karl had promised him to abolish the sectional division of the Staatsrat on his accession. Kolowrat had also warned that the finances were entering a period of severe crisis; that a change in their leadership would be very dangerous at this juncture; and that Eichhoff was the right man to direct them in these circumstances. Clam had answered that financial affairs, like any other branch of the government, needed a program approved by all ministers and that such a program was missing. Since Ludwig was expected in Ischl shortly, Clam asked Metternich how he should use these disclosures by Kolowrat when conferring with the archduke. He warned the chancellor not to allow Ludwig who indeed hated the conference to be exposed to Kolowrat's influence for any length of time.

This letter was the first indication that Eichhoff and his handling of the finances was soon to become the focal point of the political struggle. Metternich's answer [22], however, ignored this point for the moment. He promised to send Clam a letter soon, meant to be shown to Ludwig, which would expose "in very simple words" the "nullity" of Kolowrat's "divagations". He then touched upon a point that Clam must have raised often in their discussions of the political situation.

Should one man, by the side of the monarch, unite all power in his hands? Who is this man? Archduke Louis? He does not want it. I? The same. Kolowrat? He cannot do it. Baron Eichhoff? Nobody follows him! Therefore, a conseil! One may struggle against it as much as one wants, there is no other way.

Clam's next letter [23] reported how Kolowrat, "busy in all directions", tried to persuade everybody that his reform of the Staatsrat was indispensable for a quicker and more effective direction of the government. Deploring the complete lack of plan, order and discipline at court, Clam appealed to Metternich to "find a man of intelligence, tact and strong character" to direct the court. He himself had no interest in such a position which was becoming "daily a more urgent necessity of state".

This plea must have been connected with Clam's demand, a year ago, for an efficient Kabinettsdirektor for the emperor. No doubt, Clam feared that without such a reliable guardian at court Kolowrat might be able to persuade Emperor Ferdinand, with or without Ludwig's assistance or knowledge, to sign documents detrimental to Clam's and Metternich's conception of the interest of the state. Oddly enough, Metternich does not

[22] Metternich to Clam, July 23, 1837, *NP*, VI, 206.

[23] Clam to Metternich, July 23, 1837, HHSA, Staatskanzlei, K.

seem to have answered this plea, nor does the subject ever again appear in any document. Perhaps a reliable director was quickly installed.

The chancellor now asked Clam to impress on Ludwig not to change the Staatsrat in Ischl without informing him first of the proposals [24]. Clam submitted this request to Ludwig and obtained his implicit agreement. Discussing Kolowrat's hostility to the conference, Ludwig had frankly admitted his own dislike for it because the conference often did not come to the point or, if it did, degenerated into a "caterwauling". It was frequently a waste of time, the archduke had asserted, "all the more so since I understand little of politics" [25].

In another letter of the same date [26], Clam related a conversation with Franz Karl that confirmed all he had heard before about Kolowrat's plans and open propaganda for them. During a recent short visit, Archduke Johann had spent most of his time with Kolowrat and had told Franz Karl that he agreed with the minister's views about internal reforms. Johann had publicly and even demonstratively supported Kolowrat who had afterwards boasted about it. Franz Karl, Clam wrote, had answered the minister "correctly but weakly". He had promised Clam not to allow any discussion to be held, or measures taken, in Metternich's absence, and had agreed to alert Ludwig against Kolowrat's "plots".

On the subject of the Staatskonferenz, Clam begged Metternich to keep two points in mind. First, Kolowrat was determined to destroy, or at least paralyze it, mainly because he was the chancellor's junior and because Hofkammerpräsident Eichhoff hated it as a "check on his monopoly". Second, Ludwig tended to allow it to lapse into disuse because of his "monological nature", his justified doubts about its current procedure, his incomprehension of Metternicht's attempts to infuse it with "a higher spirit", and because he was under Kolowrat's influence in all internal matters.

The worst evil was not so much the existence of these opposing sentiments but the fact that none of the conference members made any attempt to resolve these differences. Clam blamed this on Ludwig's "lack of decision and cautions weakness", on Kolowrat's "deliberate duplicity", and – after protestations of undying loyalty – on Metternich's "double omission".

In the first place, Metternich had failed to take the initiative in reforming the very real defects of the conference, both in order to strengthen that institution and to weaken Kolowrat's destructive criticism. An agenda,

[24] Metternich to Clam, July 30, 1837, *NP*, VI, 206f.

[25] Clam to Metternich, August 2, 1837, HHSA, Staatskanzlei, K.

[26] Clam to Metternich, August 2, 1837, *ibid.*

proper distribution and circulation of business, and the establishment of departments were indispensable and simple reforms, rejected by Kolowrat because they would frustrate his intrigues.

In the second place, Metternich had omitted to bring "continuous, active and methodical" influence to bear on Ludwig in opposition to Kolowrat's. Since the chancellor was, for Clam, "the guarantor of the maintenance of the monarchy", he wanted him to assume a position of full power as the only possible regent. That would include his participation and initiative in all important state affairs and his absolute veto on all measures. In order to gain that position Metternich would have to reform the conference and to take the offensive in fighting the opposing party with a party of his own despite his reluctance to have one.

Metternich admitted in his answer [27] that Clam's analysis "contains the faithful picture of the truth". He explained his inactivity by the necessity "to solve the task, not to cut it". It was impossible "to drive Count Kolowrat away, since he would only reappear as a ghost". Hence "we must set to work piano". He preferred to let Kolowrat take the initiative; for the moment the only important thing was not to allow the archdukes to make any decisions at Ischl. He pointed out to Clam that the letter he sent him the day before [28] was actually meant to be shown to Ludwig. In it he had summed up his views of the situation and had described Kolowrat – despite his good qualities an "instrument" rather than a leader – as an honest man led astray by "the influence of sordid elements".

Clam's next letter reported Ludwig's explicit assurance not to take any decisive steps in Metternich's absence. Clam then implored the chancellor, once again, to end the impossible situation in which one of the two top ministers favored the conference and opposed the current financial administration, while the other abhorred the conference and was "completely dominated" by the "organ" of the finances. One of the two must win, and if the other party were to be the winner the very existence of the monarchy would be endangered. From Clam's further elaboration it is clear that he regarded Eichhoff, whose "principle opposed bluntly and irreconciliably" that of Metternich, as a more important and ruthless enemy than Kolowrat [29].

Gervay similarly described Kolowrat as intimidated and afraid of Eich-

[27] Metternich to Clam, August 6, 1837, *NP*, VI, 210.
[28] Metternich to Clam, August 5, 1837, *NP*, VI, 207-10.
[29] Clam to Metternich, August 6, 1837, HHSA, Staatskanzlei, K.

hoff whose aim was believed to be the reestablishment of the ministry of finance and the displacement of Kolowrat [30].

In another letter meant for Ludwig rather than for Clam [31], Metternich agreed that he, too, considered Eichhoff, who "terrorized" Kolowrat, the more dangerous opponent. He handled the finances as if he had "received the monarchy as a present". His aims were unclear. He would have to be brought into the daylight which he shunned to explain "what he wanted, and why and how he wanted it". Kolowrat had told Metternich that he would soon discuss the state of the finances with Eichhoff and they would then decide whether they could remain in the government. He, Metternich, had answered that he saw the problem differently: the question was whether the financial situation met the needs of the state and, if not, what measures were necessary to improve it.

The danger of an imminent *coup de main* by Kolowrat passed. The situation calmed down sufficiently to move Kübeck to the optimistic observation that while the government was weak and often arbitrary, it was "generally just, thrifty and considerate of the interest of the people ... the people are well off, in general" [32].

This mood did not last. By the end of the year both Clam and Kübeck learned that Kolowrat renewed his approaches to Franz Karl to elicit his support [33]. Bombelles regretfully noted, "Kolowrat's power and influence over Ludwig have grown stronger" [34]. Kolowrat himself made no secret of his ambition. "Only one man can rule", he told Kübeck, "it will not work without a Richelieu" [35]. Kübeck, alert to the minister's "tendency towards arbitrary power", noted in great detail how Kolowrat had arrogated railroad matters to himself after a dispute with Metternich which greatly embarrassed Ludwig [36].

Clam now resumed his effort of exhorting Metternich. On the occasion of sending him New Year's greetings, he emphasized that "the evil ... has made great progress", and expressed hope that the chancellor's "principle of order and discipline" would be victorious in the new year [37]. This was

[30] Srbik, *Metternich*, II, 23. Cf. Kübeck. *Tagebücher*, I, 759.

[31] Metternich to Clam, August 10 and 17, 1837, *NP*, VI, 210-12.

[32] Kübeck, *Tagebücher*, I, 768.

[33] *Ibid.*, 775f.

[34] Wertheimer, "Metternich und Staatskonferenz", 114; Cf. Kübeck, *Tagebücher*, I, 788.

[35] Kübeck, *Tagebücher*, I, 787.

[36] *Ibid.*, 778f.

[37] Clam to Metternich, January 1, 1838, HHSA, Staatskanzlei, K.

followed ten days later by a memorandum [38] which reiterated Clam's condemnation of the "absolutism of a cabinet-ministry" that aimed not at "great purposes of state" but instead only at the "satisfaction of petty vanities".

Metternich's weapons in fighting this evil were wrong, Clam charged with his customary frankness. They were "too noble" against a lying and treacherous enemy; "not adapted to the personality" of Ludwig, a "natural and indispensable ally"; and "not sufficiently prepared and effective" to turn the conference into a proper tool to assert the chancellor's full share of the government. It was not enough to cure a few symptons or pronounce sagacious theories. Metternich must put an end to "Eichhoff's continuous delusive tragedy of bankruptcy, and Kolowrat's comedy of indispensability", must overcome their deceit and Ludwig's indolence by correcting the latter's overestimation of Kolowrat and of Eichhoff, "the viper at our bosom".

Kübeck, to whom Clam read this memorandum before handing it to Metternich, called it, "powerful but true" [39]. It was apparently powerful enough to persuade Metternich to take the initiative at last. On January 17, 1838, he spoke at a conference session about his views of the government and further elaborated them in a memorandum he handed to the two archdukes [40]. Pointing out that a justified "feeling of discontent pervaded not only the civil service but the public at large, he demanded that inherited principles and forms be maintained, and that the "most vigorous provision" of a substitute for the weak emperor be made.

The latter function was fulfilled by the Staatskonferenz which needed to be properly organized (here Metternich quoted Clam's proposals) and whose links with the Staatsrat must be implemented in accordance with already established principles. The inherited principles and forms concerned the Staatsrat which must be maintained in that spirit because the public had confidence in its traditional advisory role. The main reason why it did not function properly was the "limited effectiveness" of the important financial section whose virtual exclusion from the examination of financial

[38] *NP*, VII, 628-31; this is incomplete, see Srbik, *Metternich*, II, 22, 24, 575 note 6 to p. 22.

[39] Kübeck, *Tagebücher*, I, 775f.

[40] "Ueber die Lage des States" vom Fürsten Metternich, undated but probably written on January 17, 1838, HHSA, Staatskanzlei, P.M.; partially printed in Schlitter, *Vormärz*, IV, 112-16.

affairs presented a "positive danger" [41]. On the other hand, the Hofkammerpräsident's participation in the discussions of his own proposals and measures made a mockery of any control of financial matters.

Metternich continued his attack on Eichhoff by denouncing the "exceptional position" of the Hofkammer which became "daily more glaringly prominent". Its president tended to act "arbitrarily and frequently terroristically" not only within his Hofstelle but also when seeking to widen his power at the expense of the rest of the civil service and of other political institutions. Metternich concluded with a strong demand for a "true and thorough liquidation" [42] in the financial field as a means of bringing "clarity and order" to it.

Archduke Ludwig was not impressed. Indeed, he told his nephew Franz Karl that he could not understand the memorandum in spite of having read it several times [43]. Somewhat discouraged, the Metternich faction continued to attack Eichhoff. Clam sent the chancellor a list of useful points to be made in the conference about Eichhoff's handling of the finances. They elaborated Metternich's complaints about the insufficient participation in government business by the Staatsrat in general and the financial section in particular [44].

When the budget was discussed in the conference, early in March 1838, Metternich insisted that Eichhoff must render account for his past financial management and submit a program for the future. He also wanted financial affairs discussed in the conference with the participation by appropriate Staatsräte (most of whom loathed Eichhoff). Kolowrat conceded both points after several days of maneuvering, but it was no victory at all for Metternich since he had been outwitted in both instances. On the first point, instead of a written order, Eichhoff was instructed to discuss "the true meaning of his demand" with Metternich. Nor was there any written arrangement for the second point, in order to avoid tying Ludwig's hands [45]. A few days later Kolowrat complained to Kübeck that Metternich interfered

[41] Metternich called this "a direct deviation from the system", but, while undoubtedly deplorable, it was clearly sanctioned by the settlement of December 12, 1836.

[42] It was, as Kübeck said, "an unhappy terminology" (*Tagebücher*, I, 781, 786). "Liquidation" in German means "settlement", but Metternich used the term in the sense of "clarification, clearing up a situation". Cf. *NP*, VI, 216.

[43] Wertheimer, "Metternich und Staatskonferenz", 114.

[44] Clam's "Baron Eichhoff'sche Finanzwirtschaft", February 3, 1838, HHSA, Staatskanzlei, P.M.

[45] Kübeck, *Tagebücher*, I, 781, 784-86.

in everything while understanding less than a district clerk of financial matters [46].

Once more nothing had changed. But while the power of the Kolowrat faction was undiminished, Metternich's influence in the conference began to wane. Franz Karl still supported him loyally and assured Princess Melanie that nothing could move him from the straight path "and the straight path is Prince Metternich" [47]. Ludwig, however, Kübeck noted in March, "had changed his position". He had succumbed sufficiently to the influence of the "Eichhoff-Kolowrat" party to believe that any attack on them was directed at his own authority. "Where is this going to lead us?" Kübeck asked despondently [48].

[46] *Ibid.*, 787.

[47] *Ibid.*, 784f.; *NP*, VI, 223.

[48] Kübeck, *Tagebücher*, I, 784f.

CHAPTER XVII

JUSTAMENTNICHT-REGIEREN

After 1838 the conference hardly ever met in regular sessions. Ludwig and Kolowrat almost never attended, thus reducing its procedure to written reports and decisions. Ludwig increasingly adopted Emperor Franz's favorite "Kabinettsweg", the ultimate perversion of orderly government [1]. Tension between the two rivals was "stronger than ever", Kübeck reported when yet another reform scheme by Kolowrat had failed, early in 1839 [2]. The latter still employed what Kübeck called "the worn-out, ridiculous threat of resignation" with "unvaryingly incredible success" to impose his will on Ludwig. In at least one instance he thus enforced a currupt government contract concluded by Eichhoff [3].

The government functioned as slowly and as ineffectively as ever. "4,000 documents are piling up on Archduke Ludwig's desk, and neither he nor Count Sedlnitzky can be persuaded to deal with the arrears", Kolowrat told Hofrat Hammer [4]. Metternich was no less guilty in his eyes. The chancellor, he charged, "gets nowhere because he talks too much and Archduke Ludwig does not dare to interrupt this babble" [5]. Already some years earlier, Kolowrat had expressed dissatisfaction with Metternich's talkativeness in conferences [6]. As the latter turned older, he seems to have displayed an increasing tendency to turn conversations into monologues [7]. Undoubtedly Kolowrat's irritation was justified when he complained to Kübeck in 1839:

[1] Wertheimer, "Metternich und Staatskonferenz", 121, 125; Srbik, *Metternich*, II, 26.
[2] Kübeck, *Tagebücher*, I, 805.
[3] *Ibid.*, 807.
[4] Hammer-Purgstall, *Erinnerungen*, 331.
[5] *Ibid.*, 327.
[6] Kübeck, *Tagebücher*, I, 537, 617.
[7] Springer, *Geschichte*, I, 559; Srbik, *Metternich*, I, 261, 268f.

Prince Metternich and I, we both mean well and I greatly respect his intelligence and character, but we can never understand each other. The prince always adopts a lecturing manner with me, he tells me that 5 and 3 is only 8, but 5 times 3 is 15, that there is a great difference between the words "then" and "once" which the government must keep in mind, that all events are interconnected, hence the opium war between the Chinese and the English cannot remain without consequence for our finances, etc. etc. And he tells me all this when I asked him if he agreed to grant the Northern Railroad a new line to Pressburg. Add to this the insufferable vanity of a man who was never wrong in his life, who has foretold and foreseen all that happened and did not happen – in short, with whom I cannot walk [8].

Perhaps Metternich's loquacity vis-à-vis Kolowrat was due to his own irritation and growing despair at his total exclusion from internal affairs and inability to reform the government. One week after the outbreak of the revolution of 1848, he explained the situation to Count Ficquelmont:

My department and I myself have represented the Austrian power to the outside world, while a vacuum established itself in the interior. I have thus become (which I find morally repugnant) a phantasmagoria, an imaginary being, a spirit without body, a representative of what should have existed but existed no longer [9].

After his severe illness in the autumn of 1839, his wife noted that he was reluctant to deal with internal matters where he met only unpleasantness and opposition "that are destroying him in the end. He no longer has the necessary strength to fight". Two weeks later she added, "he feels too old to fight, he no longer trusts himself to have the strength" [10].

But even before his illness his supporters had become concerned about his inactivity which they considered neither masterly nor wise. Princess Melanie recorded a conversation with Clam, in the summer of 1838, in which he expressed his conviction that one word from Metternich would remove their enemies, and his dismay at his not saying that word. Bombelles, too, was certain the chancellor would win once he took up the fight against Kolowrat in earnest. Archduke Franz Karl similarly complained that Metternich was not forceful enough against his enemies [11].

Clam continued to appeal to his "intellectual, moral and worldhistorical superiority" [12]. After his illness he sent him a "sketch for a memorandum on what is necessary for us" [13]. Only Metternich through his moral power,

[8] Kübeck, *Tagebücher*, I, 846f.

[9] *NP*, VII, 612.

[10] *NP*, VI, 368.

[11] *NP*, VI, 226, 232; Wertheimer, "Metternich und Staatskonferenz", 122.

[12] Srbik, *Metternich*, II, 26.

[13] Clam to Metternich, September 29, 1839, HHSA, Staatskanzlei, K.

Clam maintained, could remedy the "notorious condition" of the conference by demanding a return to oral deliberation, the assistance of competent Referenten, and the inclusion of financial questions.

This was probably Clam's last contribution. Four months later he died. His death saddened and discouraged Metternich deeply [14]. His authority was now so shaky that his supporters feared that Kolowrat would seize the military section of the Staatsrat and thus control the army which Clam had called "the only symbol of unity and power in Austria" [15]. Clam's successor as head of section D, a military nonentity, was described as an "honest good worker but not a fighter by nature", by Bombelles who gloomily forecast Kolowrat's domination of the army by financial manipulation [16].

After Clam's death, Archduchess Sophie took up for a time his exertions to rouse Metternich to a confrontation with Kolowrat whose elimination she saw as essential to resolve all conflicts and to advance her husband. Despite her assurances that at the decisive moments Ludwig would take the chancellor's side against Kolowrat, her efforts were unsuccessful. When she asked Metternich why he did not get rid of his rival, he answered, "one must let him die off, but one must not kill him". Bombelles who reported this conversation added regretfully, "he has been saying that for five years, but the other one is tougher than he is". Hartig as well as Ficquelmont, who had been called to Vienna during Metternich's illness to assist him at the Staatskanzlei with the rank of Staats- und Konferenzminister, now joined the chorus of those imploring Metternich to reform the conference [17].

The chancellor himself was aware of the urgency to establish a strong central government in the face of growing nationalism. "Where there is no Centrum, everything at the periphery must fall to pieces", he wrote to Gervay [18]. Yet his invariable answer to all exhortations was "let us keep quiet. We are right and time helps those who are right and harms those who are wrong" [19].

The only result of all these pressures was Metternich's instruction to Kübeck to send him his "frank" views on forming a regency. The Staatsrat

[14] *NP*, VI, 370 f.

[15] Wertheimer, "Metternich und Staatskonferenz", 117; Kübeck, *Tagebücher*, I, 777.

[16] Wertheimer, "Metternich und Staatskonferenz", 118f.

[17] Wertheimer, "Metternich und Staatskonferenz", 118-20.

[18] Walter, "Metternich-Gervay Briefwechsel", 243.

[19] Kübeck, *Tagebücher*, I, 808. Kübeck added, "but time also sanctifies the wrong and ennobles the bad". (*Ibid.*).

complied with a letter that was both frank and discreet [20]. He saw his task as the creation of a "regency without giving it the name or the appearance of one, and without differentiating it from existing and traditional forms". According to the "organism" created in the autumn of 1836, the regency had three branches: (1) a regent – Ludwig, as deputy of the emperor; (2) a regency-council – the Staatskonferenz, with the function of governing; (3) a central administration-council – the Staatsrat, to control the administration.

Kübeck found this basic scheme "excellent" but its execution poor. To make Ludwig the president of the conference had been the crucial error. Representing the sovereign, the right of final decision should have been reserved for him after receiving the opinions of his councils. Apart from the "venerated personality of the prince", as Kübeck delicately put it, a regent cannot be included in a lively discussion without either compromising his own hasty opinions or suppressing the freedom of deliberation. The result of this error was the elimination of the conference from important matters and the "almost timid avoidance ... of oral deliberations".

Having thus posed the problem in a different context to that of Clam and Metternich, Kübeck returned to their interpretation by supporting their demand for the setting up of a firm procedure for the Staatskonferenz, and for a regulation of its relation to the Staatsrat which lacked the guiding influence that it should receive from the conference.

As a solution, Kübeck proposed to give the three branches a connecting link that would be above "all quarrels about rank, and jealousies". Franz Karl should be placed "at the head of both conference and Staatsrat" in such a way that "all business would be concentrated on him and reach Archduke Ludwig only from him". Kübeck saw several advantages in these arrangements: an easing of Ludwig's work-load, unity and agreement in the government, support for the government by Franz Karl in a position that need not be publicized, and finally a better future for the state if the heir-apparent was now introduced to active participation in the government. Two minor proposals were clearly meant as sops to Metternich. He was to be given a copy of the agendas of all Hofstellen to keep him informed of all business. Franz Karl was to have an assistant who possessed the chancellor's confidence.

It was a sensible plan that would probably have improved the government, but it did not touch upon the basic problem of the rivalry. This was

[20] Kübeck to Metternich, February 3, 1840, HHSA, Staatsrat, Praes., Kart. 4; printed in *OZV*, 285-90.

no doubt one reason why Metternich rejected it but it was not the only one. In the first place, he did not share Kübeck's favorable opinion of Franz Karl's ability [21]. Once, when about to consult the archduke *pro forma* about some appointment, Metternich predicted, "he will have no opinion whatever" [22]. Princess Melanie, who in all such matters faithfully reflected her husband's views, called Franz Karl "incapable, without a true character" [23]. After the revolution, defending Metternich's insistence on Ferdinand's legitimate succession, she pointed to Franz Karl's "miserable character" and contended that his accession would have led to a surer and prompter ruin [24].

Metternich's fear of rivalry between Ludwig and Franz Karl, and of the latter's susceptibility to the influence of his uncles Carl and Johann, and even more to that of Kolowrat who just then revived one of his schemes to put Franz Karl in charge of a commission to clear up government arrears – all these elements contributed to his opposition to Kübeck's plan. In the same way he continued to reject all successive attempts by Sophie and by Franz Karl himself to make the archduke head of the Staatsrat or the conference. Since Ludwig, too, opposed these projects, they were doomed to failure [25].

There were some partial victories for Metternich in the early forties. By June 1838 both Clam and Kübeck noticed that Kolowrat had begun to drop Eichhoff [26]. When the latter proved unable to cure the growing deficit and increasingly came into conflict with the highest officials on financial policies, he was finally completely isolated and had to resign in November 1840 [27]. Kübeck's appointment as his successor as Hofkammerpräsident was of great benefit to both Metternich and the state, but even his ability, honesty and expert knowledge could do little to raise the finances

[21] Kübeck attributed "intelligence, heart and good will" to Franz Karl (*Tagebücher*, I, 680). On the other hand, he reported the Tsar's remark at Teplitz that the archduke "looked as if he had not matured. If he were only eighteen one could be hopeful; but since he is past thirty one must despair". (*Ibid.*, 700).

[22] Friedrich Walter, "Der Rücktritt Graf Carl Choteks vom Oberstburggrafenamte und die Ernennung Erzherzogs Stephans zum Landeschef in Böhmen", *Mitteilungen des Vereins für Geschichte der Deutschen in Böhmen*, LX (1922), 170.

[23] Srbik, *Metternich*, II, 571, note 4 to p. 7. Omitted in *NP*, VII, 145.

[24] Schlitter, *Vormärz*, IV, 118f. Omitted in *NP*, VIII.

[25] Wertheimer, "Metternich und Staatskonferenz", 119-121; Srbik, *Metternich*, II, 26f.; Walter, *Zentralverwaltung*, 201.

[26] Kübeck, *Tagebücher*, I, 794.

[27] Walter, *Zentralverwaltung*, 266; Schlitter, *Vormärz*, IV, 116; Adolf Beer, *Die Finanzen Oesterreichs im 19. Jahrhundert* (Prague: Tempsky, 1877), 145-50.

from the dismal state to which a decade of the Kolowrat-Eichhoff regime had brought them, not least because the conference buried or crippled his most important measures [28].

The transfer of Count Hartig in the same year to Vienna from his governorship in Milan to head the political section of the Staatsrat, further reinforced the Metternich camp. Hartig almost immediately pressed for a return to oral discussion in the Staatsrat and succeeded in having amendments to the instructions issued to that effect, but – as so often before – within eighteen months vested interests and old habits managed to return to the old written procedure [29].

All three of the "new" men – Ficquelmont, Hartig and Kübeck – could not quite compensate for the loss of Clam's drive and prestige. The first two, however, continued his pressure on Metternich to reform the Staatskonferenz. To appease them the chancellor introduced a kind of "*Vorkonferenz*" (pre-conference) in which he and Kolowrat, assisted by a few experts (chiefly Kübeck and Hartig) discussed subjects that were to be sent to the conference. Whatever useful purpose this pre-conference may have had, it contributed to a further weakening of the conference itself. Anything that Metternich and Kolowrat were able to agree upon, the inexperienced Franz Karl was unlikely to oppose and Ludwig was only too happy to sign. The problem, as ever, was harmony among the rivals. However, the Vorkonferenz soon fell into disuse when Sophie and Franz Karl clamored for the latter's participation, a demand that could not be granted without arousing Ludwig's suspicion and jealousy [30].

A last attempt to breathe life into the conference was initiated by Kübeck who intended to make it, through participation of the presidents of the Hofstellen (of whom he was one), into a "*Ministerrat*" (council ofministers), the central point of the government". He won Metternich over for this plan, and he in turn persuaded both Ludwig and Kolowrat to agree to it. Early in December 1843 detailed instructions for the Staatskonferenz were at last issued [31], providing it – seven years after its creation – with the proper procedure Clam had urged so strongly. The conference was to meet once a week, to deliberate orally, and was granted initiative in selecting its subjects.

Once again, as so many times before, a new and hopeful beginning seemed to have been made; and once again, as so many times before, these

[28] Beer, *Finanzen*, 151f.

[29] Walter, *Zentralverwaltung*, 158-60.

[30] Wertheimer, "Metternich und Staatskonferenz", 122.

[31] Printed in *OZV*, 290-92.

hopes were quickly disappointed. Within six weeks Kübeck had to admit that his effort was "a still-born child". The conference simply did not meet. The cause of failure seems to have been Ludwig's objection to submit himself to the weekly ordeal of a conference session [32].

In May 1842 Metternich wrote to Kübeck: "*Nobody governs today*, nor is there a firm basis for the *administration*" [33]. The Viennese called this lack of government "*Justamentnicht-regieren*" (now-less-than-ever-non-governing) [34]. In the same year, Andrian declared in his book, "things cannot remain in Austria as they are now ..." [35]. No further efforts were made by anybody to reform the government. The rest, while not exactly silence, was a slow, almost fatalistic drift towards the explosion of 1848 [36]. The motto of Count Eduard Taaffe, the Austrian Prime Minister of the eighteen-eighties, might be applied to the last few years of Vormärz Austria: "*immer fortwurschteln*" (just muddling through).

[32] Wertheimer, "Metternich und Staatskonferenz", 124f.; Kübeck, *Tagebücher*, II, 11f.

[33] Beer, "Kübeck und Metternich", 29.

[34] Frankl, *Erinnerungen*, 231.

[35] Andrian, *Oesterreich und dessen Zukunft*, 167.

[36] In 1846 Princess Melanie recorded a Viennese joke about a conference discussion on the unrest in Galicia. Archduke Albrecht said: "I have enough soldiers and cannon, one must shoot, execute, etc.". Archduke Ludwig protested: "That is not possible, everything must go through proper channels and then come before the Staatsrat and conference". Archduke Franz Karl: "I agree with everything. But I insist that Pokorny must at last be made director of the Theater beim Kärntner Thor". The emperor: "I did not know that Tarnow belongs to me". Melanie added sadly that this malicious invention unfortunately presented a true picture of the government. Metternich, incidentally, as well as Kolowrat are missing in this version. (Srbik, *Metternich*, II, 589, note 6 to p. 181. Omitted in *NP*, VII, 145).

CHAPTER XVIII

REFORMING AUTOCRACIES

As we have seen, Metternich persistently attempted to reform the Austrian government by emancipating ministries from the irresponsible collegiate board system [1] and from the restriction of territorial considerations into hierarchically organized *Fachministerien* (specialized departments), headed by responsible ministers. Dazzled by Napoleon's great example, he at first stressed the Staatsrat as the principal governmental institution. Soon, however, even before Kolowrat's advent, he neglected the Staatsrat in favor of a ministerial conference.

What brought about this change of emphasis? It seems likely that two considerations of a personal nature must have been in his mind. In the first place, he cannot have seen much scope for himself in a Staatsrat of the kind he envisaged. He could neither, in good conscience, advocate a Staatsrat with different functions or structure, nor pervert its purpose for his own personal ends as Kolowrat did.

The second consideration concerned the personality of Emperor Franz. In this connection it is instructive to view Metternich's plans in the context of the general political climate of the time which favored governmental reform under the stress of war and revolution. A comparison of the reforms effected or contemplated by the other three great autocracies of Europe will illuminate the intentions of Metternich who, after all, explicitly mentioned two of their examples [2].

When the Abbé Sieyès drew up his constitutional proposals on the morrow of the coup d'état of 1799, he provided for an extreme division of

[1] The eighteenth century collegiate principle of administration in Austria, Prussia and Russia was everywhere felt to be responsible for delay and confusion. Cf. Marc Raeff, *Michael Speransky* (The Hague: Martinus Nijhoff, 1957), 107, 130 and Max Lehmann, *Freiherr vom Stein* (Leipzig: S. Hirzel, 1902), II, 370f.

[2] See above, p. 28.

powers. Legislative functions were to be distributed between three assemblies, executive power between a Grand Elector, a senate and two consuls. The purpose of this complicated structure was to protect the individual against the despotism of the state. Napoleon, however, insisted on executive power for himself alone. The resulting "compromise", the constitution of the year VIII, made him omnipotent. His officials were responsible to no one except the conseil d'état whose members he appointed. He regarded his ministers only as glorified department heads executing his commands, never permitted to stray beyond the confines of their departments or to act in unison [3].

When Sieyès revived the *conseil du roi* in the form of a new conseil d'état, he probably meant to give it some power of decision. Napoleon turned it into an advisory body of technicians and specialists, providing expert assistance in the drafting of laws and administrative regulations under his own direction [4].

Divided into five or six sections, its thirty to fifty members had no initiative but were charged with translating Napoleon's ideas through oral deliberation into legislative form with speed and efficiency [5]. Its brilliance outshone all other institutions. It was not only a "laboratory of laws" but also "of men" [6]. Napoleon chose the best brains of his time as councillors and used the council as a nursery of administrators for its junior members, the maîtres des requêtes and auditeurs. Frequently presiding in person, he encouraged free speech and provoked lively debates. The council owed much of its lustre and success to Napoleon's analytical mind and penetrating intelligence [7].

Alexander I, introduced by his grandmother Catherine II to the philosophes and inspired by the example of Napoleon's popular dictatorship, took the first steps in reforming the Russian government immediately after his accession in 1801. He set up departmental ministries and replaced the old "all-highest council" with a council of state without, however,

[3] Georges Lefebvre, *Napoléon* (3rd ed. Paris: Presses Universitaires de France, 1947), 69-71.

[4] Charles Durand, *Études sur le conseil d'état Napoléonien* (Paris: Presses Universitaires de France, 1949), 59-63.

[5] Maurice Deslandres, *Histoire Constitutionelle de la France* (Paris: Librairie Armand Colin, 1932), I, 451-53.

[6] Louis Madelin, *The Consulate and the Empire*, trans. E.F. Buckley (New York: Putnam's Sons, 1934), 283.

[7] "What struck me most [about Napoleon]", wrote Metternich, "was the remarkable insight and great simplicity of his mind". (*NP*, I, 277).

clearly defining its scope or structure [8]. In 1803 Michael Speransky, then a relatively minor official, complained in a memorandum on reform that ministers could escape the consequences of arbitrary actions by claiming to be a "physical extension" of the tsar. He advocated as a basic principle the separation of legislative from executive power, and within the latter, administrative from judicial functions [9].

In 1813, one year after his dismissal, he was to explain the aim of his reforms to have been the establishment "of the government, hitherto aristocratic, on a basis of inviolable law". A separation of powers [10] was essential but must be "sincere and real" and not, as in France, a mere legal cover for autocracy; it must limit sovereign power "by facts and not by words". His plan, thus designed to turn Russia into a constitutional monarchy, had been – not surprisingly – largely rejected by Alexander [11].

Speransky's reform plan of 1809 attempted, in his own words, "to regularize power by law and to ensure administration by rules and institutions". He proposed to create a State *Duma*, an advisory body of limited functions, representative at best of local dumas, similar to western Estates. He wanted to preserve the senate as the highest institution of judicial review and appeal, and intended to reorganize the ministries in such a way that the ministers would become "responsible" by "harmonizing their actions with the true spirit of the existing laws". The legislative, judicial and executive powers thus separated were to be united in the person of the sovereign, assisted by an advisory Council of State which was modelled largely on Napoleon's yet mindful of Russian eighteenth century forerunners [12].

Speransky's proposals were quite conservative. Even where he ventured into the field of representation, only landowners were to be enfranchized in indirect elections. Yet only two of his measures were enacted. The rest of his proposals were amended and debated into oblivion by influential opponents hostile to reform and foreign influence. Speransky succeeded

[8] Eric Amburger, *Geschichte der Behördenorganisation Russlands von Peter dem Grossen bis 1917* (Leiden: E.J. Brill, 1966), 23-25, 65f.

[9] Raeff, *Speransky*, 108; Boris Nolde, "L'autocratie Russe et la doctrine de la séparation des pouvoirs dans la première moitié du XIXe siècle", *Revue du Droit Public*, XLI (1924), 20-22.

[10] Speransky's – like Metternich's – concept of separation of powers had nothing to do with checks and balances but only with greater efficiency. Cf. Raeff, *Speransky*, 141, and above, p. 32.

[11] Nolde, "L'autocratie", 23-27.

[12] Raeff, *Speransky*, 133-41, 156-58.

in reorganizing the ministries on the basis of clear delineation of jurisdiction and proper rules of procedure. Their heads, reduced to purely executive and administrative functions, became responsible to the emperor; the old collegiate board system was at last abolished [13].

The Council of State which was to bring "order and uniformity in governmental affairs" was divided into five departments. The tsar, who appointed ministers and other high officials as its members, was its president but a State Secretary – Speransky himself was the first one – directed its deliberation and agenda. It was charged with drafting laws but was not given any initiative in this field. In addition to its primary function of legislative advice the Council quickly acquired a judicial role, dealing with cases which the senate could not settle. Speransky protested in vain to Alexander against this departure from his plan and it was mainly this aspect of the Council that led Metternich to dismiss it as an example for his Staatsrat [14].

The story of governmental reform in Prussia is complicated by the disagreement between the two chief reformers. Where Karl vom Stein advocated decentralization as a curb on royal absolutism, Karl August von Hardenberg favored centralization in order to guide absolutism. The chief aim of both was power and efficiency in the government. But while Stein, emotional and passionate, was prepared to grant the citizens a role in the provincial administration in order to arouse their patriotism, Hardenberg, like Metternich a product of eighteenth century rationalism, proposed to apply the ideas of the French revolution to Prussia through a revolution from above. He intended "to destroy everywhere powerless and anachronistic institutions". The formula "most appropriate to the present Zeitgeist" seemed to him to be "democratic principles in a monarchical government" [15].

The Prussian "cabinet", a private, unofficial body of four high officials most of whom both Stein and Hardenberg considered ineffective and corrupt, was generally blamed for the catastrophe of Jena and Auerstädt. Stein accused the members of the cabinet, as Speransky had accused the Russian ministers, of deliberating and making decisions "without responsibility" since "the king's person sanctions their proceedings" and others

[13] Michael T. Florinsky, *Russia, a History and an Interpretation* (New York: Macmillan, 1964), II, 696-98.

[14] Metternich rejected the Russian example as unsuitable for Austria because its function was "the organization of a new country" and because it was "in many respects an Oberste Justizstelle and an Oberste Rechencontrolle". (*OZV*, 191).

[15] Ernst Meier, *Die Reform der Verwaltungsorganisation unter Stein und Hardenberg* (Leipzig: Dunker & Humblot, 1881), 139-45; 166-70; Walter M. Simon, *The Failure of the Prussian Reform Movement 1807-1819* (Ithaca: Cornell University Press, 1955), 52f.

had to execute their policy. In a letter to King Friedrich Wilhelm III in 1806, Stein called the cabinet "a power without assigned competence, without responsibility, interfering everywhere and directing nothing" [16].

When the king called him to office in 1807, Stein revived the eighteenth century Staatsrat as a cabinet-ministry, a conference of departmental ministers, royal princes, Staatsräte and other high officials. Divided into five executive departments and meeting in regular and frequent sessions under the presidency of the king, it was charged with drawing up legislation and with the control of the administration, and possessed a certain amount of executive power. It essentially fulfilled Stein's aim of modifying royal power without tying down the king by majority decisions. As Gerhard Ritter points out, the deliberate equalization of ministers with their subordinates in the spirit of the collegiate system of the old *Generaldirektorium* (analoguous to the Austrian Hofstellen) was intended to curb political tendencies of the ministers [17].

After Stein's dismissal in 1810 and the failure of the Dohna-Altenstein ministry, Hardenberg became Staatskanzler. Where Stein had preferred the "predominant influence", as he put it, of a president of the Staatsrat to a strong Minister Presidency, Hardenberg's reform created a powerful Staatskanzler, responsible directly for internal and financial affairs, and indirectly controlling all other ministries. The Staatsrat increasingly lost power and influence and was reduced to an advisory status on legislation [18].

Efficiency was thus the primary aim of the governmental reforms in all four autocracies. All favored the rule of law over arbitrary action, both for its own sake and even more in order to increase their governments' efficacy. Hence they provided – though Prussia to a much lesser degree – a measure of separation of legislative and administrative powers. Delineation of spheres of action, definitions of the powers and functions of institutions, and modernization of bureaucratic procedures – all were meant to contribute to efficiency.

[16] J.R. Seeley, *Life and Times of Stein* (Cambridge: University Press, 1878), I, 267-73, 280f.; Otto Hintze, "Die Entstehung der modernen Staatsministerien", *Historische Zeitschrift*, C (1908), 86; Meier, *Reform*, 178.

[17] Meier, *Reform*, 177f., 182-88; Ernst Meier, *Französische Einflüsse auf die Staats- und Rechtentwicklung Preussens im XIX. Jahrhundert* (Leipzig: Dunker & Humblot, 1908), II, 306-08; Gerhard Ritter, *Stein, eine politische Biographie* (Stuttgart: Deutsche Verlagsanstalt, 1931), I, 373f.

[18] Hintze, "Entstehung der Staatsministerien", 103f.; Lehmann, *Stein*, II, 371-73; Meier, "Französische Einflüsse", II, 417-23.

None of the councils of state had more than advisory powers, none imposed any effective limitation on the will of the monarch. Hence where the sovereign was a genius the government worked well; where he was erratic, mediocre or narrow-minded, it did not.

Metternich must have recognized that a Staatsrat advising a second-rate monarch, to say nothing of a weakminded one, could only be of limited importance. He therefore proposed to supplement the sole point of unity in the government, the person of the emperor, by a ministerial conference headed by himself in order to provide more effective and authoritative advice to the emperor.

CHAPTER XIX

METTERNICH'S FAILURE

Throughout his forty years in office Metternich was always aware of the defects of the Austrian government. He diagnosed its sickness as a confusion of administration with government and as a consequent overburdening of the emperor and the Staatsrat with trivial problems. His reform proposals had two objectives. First, he insisted on the separation of policy making from administration. The government, he believed, should be strengthened at the center while the administration should be concentrated in the provinces, respecting the historical and cultural individuality of the crownlands.

Secondly, he advocated a "distribution of powers" within the government. The Staatsrat was to control the administration while a conference of ministers with departmental responsibilities was to be the highest organ of the government. Metternich also sought to replace the government's cumbersome written procedure by oral discussion. Emperor Franz's narrow-minded jealousy of his prerogatives, his petty bureaucratism and morbid aversion to change destroyed any effectiveness his half-hearted acceptance of some of Metternich's proposals might have produced.

The arrival of Kolowrat subtly changed Metternich's attitude to reform without affecting its basic principles. The aims of internal reform and rivalry in the power struggle now largely coincided. It was more important than ever to define precisely the functions and spheres of activity of the various institutions in order to curb Kolowrat's domination of the Staatsrat and his predominant influence in the government. If Emperor Franz had been indecisive and obstinate, Archduke Ludwig was indecisive and weak. Kolowrat's unscrupulous ambition and sabotage of all orderly procedure carried the day and condemned the government to function as slowly and as ineffectively as ever.

It is unlikely that Metternich's reform plans, had they been put into effect, would have radically altered the course of Austrian history. They would certainly have fulfilled his expectation of strengthening the government by increasing its efficiency and adapting it to the faster pulse of the nineteenth century. But none of his proposals was, or was meant to be, designed to bring about any greater political change than the devolution of power from sovereign to minister.

They preserved the conservative character of a government hostile to new social and, to some extent, economic forces. Metternich regarded the bourgeoisie as a disruptive element of society which had to be restrained. Nor would he make more than cultural and administrative concessions to awakening national consciousness.

Thus neither liberal nor national aspirations would have been allowed any political expression. Hence even a more rationally organized, more vigorous and effective government would have been unable to avoid or withstand the explosion of 1848. Yet his reform projects were desirable and – within their limits – progressive. They would have enabled the monarchy to fulfil better the heavy tasks his foreign policy imposed upon it and might have taken the edge off the incipient nationalism.

"I have perhaps governed Europe occasionally, but never Austria", Metternich may or may not have said. Why did he not govern Austria? Why did he fail to achieve the power that would seem to have been within his grasp, or fail even to reform the government? That was a modest enough ideal on which nearly all Austrian statesmen of the period were in principle agreed.

Metternich himself had several answers. "I did not govern the empire", he wrote to his daughter in 1849, "I only directed its foreign policy. The truth is the empire did not have a government" [1]. In a letter to Hartig, a few months earlier, he had sounded the same note: "The principal evil consisted in '*non-governing*' and its consequence was the confusion of *administration* with '*governing*'!" [2]. The chief author of this confusion was Emperor Franz, he charged [3], and ever since 1814 "all my demands of the government had the fate of a voice in the desert" [4].

The chancellor admitted that his rivalry with Kolowrat "contributed substantially" to the outbreak of the revolution. Hartig and Ficquelmont agreed with him that disunity in the Staatskonferenz was the main cause

[1] *NP*, VIII, 204.
[2] *Metternich-Hartig Briefwechsel*, 22.
[3] Wertheimer, "Metternich und Staatskonferenz", 48; *NP*, VII, 617.
[4] *NP*, VIII, 225.

of the debacle [5]. The chief reason why this rivalry was allowed to develop to such significant proportions was its early encouragement by Emperor Franz and the later absence of a strong restraining hand by the emperor or the regent. In 1842 Metternich wrote to Gervay, "our illness is the lack of command from the throne and this is a great evil" [6]. A few days before the revolution Metternich explained his impotence to Hübner:

With us, as in all monarchies, a minister is only strong as far as he can count on the support of his sovereign. Just because Archduke Ludwig, the deputy of Emperor Ferdinand, is not the sovereign he cannot give me any assistance. Hence I had to fight alone against my opponents whose head, nominally, is Kolowrat. I am paralyzed since the change of rule [7].

This is an unsatisfactory argument. The chancellor was almost equally paralyzed – in internal matters – when he had Emperor Franz's strong if restricted support, and Ludwig's failure was not due to his position as regent but to his weak character.

Why did he not use the threat of resignation? Did he really cling to office for his own benefit, acceding to a policy (or the lack of one) that he knew would lead to disaster, as Bibl asserted in his anti-Srbik polemic? [8] It is true that Metternich was afraid his offer of resignation would be accepted by Emperor Franz or even be called for if he disagreed too strongly with the emperor's policies or prejudices [9]; and he probably feared a similar fate at the hand of Ludwig who in the last eight years before the revolution began to treat him with increasing coldness [10]. Bombelles, in 1840, thought the threat would be successful, but if it failed "it would be more honorable to retire than to be a witness and hence a promoter of our ruin" [11].

Metternich did not share this view. "The world still needs me because ... nobody can replace me", he wrote to his son in 1828 when he sincerely believed himself indispensable to the peace and order of Europe [12]. After

[5] *NP*, VII, 619; Hartig, *Genesis*, 37; Ludwig von Ficquelmont, *Aufklärungen* (Leipzig: Barth, 1850), 2f.; cf. Schmidt, *Zeitgenössige Geschichte*, 525.

[6] Walter, "Rücktritt Choteks", 171.

[7] Hübner, *Ein Jahr*, 14.

[8] Bibl, *Dämon*, 403.

[9] See above, p. 15. Since this statement to the Russian general was meant to assure the Tsar that Metternich did not dictate foreign policy to his emperor at a time when Austria opposed Russian adventures in the Balkans, it should perhaps be taken with a grain of salt. But in view of Franz's character and obsession with his prerogatives, Metternich's fear seems fully justified.

[10] Wertheimer, "Metternich und Staatskonferenz", 117.

[11] *Ibid.*

[12] *NP*, IV, 414.

Emperor Franz's death he feared his departure would precipitate the revolution. "My resignation would cause the collapse of the building ... [it] is synonymous with the revolution" [13], he told Hübner who years later remarked: "Grown together with the political edifice" since the first decade of the century, his resignation was to him "equivalent to a change of incalculable consequence" [14]. Perhaps Metternich's reluctance to use this form of pressure was also to some extent due to his repeated scornful condemnations of Kolowrat for abusing this weapon.

Metternich was not a fighter by nature. He preferred to let time fight his battles for him. He believed that time was on his side – "time helps those who are right" – and until the time was right one had to submit to "the force of things". Hence it was better not to kill the enemy but to "let him die off". In 1834 he told Prokesch-Osten: "All skill lies in moderation. Every illness must end; it is a matter of surviving it. One can do this by sparing one's vital energies" [15]. After his own grave illness at the age of sixty-seven in 1839, his vital energies were low and his wife thought him too weak to fight. These explanations, basing his reluctance to enter the fray on philosophical tenets or physical weakness, are not convincing and seem perilously close to rationalizations.

Metternich's correspondence with Gervay in 1843 gives a revealing glimpse of his aversion to fight for his convictions. The chancellor strongly opposed the appointment of Archduke Stephan, son of the palatine Joseph, as governor of Bohemia because he regarded him as incompetent. But although both Archdukes Ludwig and Franz Karl were equally critical of this "dangerous" and "absurd" nomination, and no decision had yet been made in the conference, Metternich considered the appointment an "evil which I am unable to prevent". He merely hoped to modify its consequences with the aid of Kübeck and Hartig. This renunciation is all the more surprising in view of his belief that Kolowrat, who had advocated the nomination, was being used by Stephan and the Bohemian nationalists for their own purposes. Significantly, he asked Gervay to burn the letter in which he had written all this.

A few days later he returned to the subject, still objecting to the appointment because provinces administered by archdukes tended to be removed from the power of the central government. This was "in the nature of things ... inevitable". Stephan's nomination could indeed be fought, he

[13] Hübner, *Ein Jahr*, 14.

[14] *NP*, VIII, 625.

[15] Prokesch-Osten, *Tagebücher*, 225.

admitted, but was the fight desirable? "Can one guarantee its success?" [16]. Thus a fight, even for the right principles, was desirable only if victory was likely, nay, guaranteed.

When Metternich returned to the Staatskanzlei from Emperor Franz's death-bed, he told his physician: "Ferdinand is emperor". Dr. Jäger answered: "Richelieu, then" [17]. But the chancellor always maintained that he did not want supreme power. "I have never discovered the stuff in me, nor felt the temptation, to become a Richelieu", he told Hübner; and he added, "Austria, just because of the multiplicity of its nationalities, can not suffer a *maire du palais*" [18]. Political principles thus confirmed personal reasons. It is not clear which of these he referred to when he wrote to Clam that he did not want to "unite all power in his hands" [19].

His repeated objections to the office of Prime Minister seem similarly based on a combination of political expedients and precepts. On the one hand he tried to prevent his rivals from seizing the power of a Prime Minister *de jure* or *de facto* – though in the case of Wallis he deliberately exaggerated that danger in order to persuade Emperor Franz of the error of his constitutional ideas. On the other hand he asserted the principle that the power of a Prime Minister could only be based on the weakness of a monarch or a regent. One cannot fail, however, to detect an element of rationalization here too, in view of the determined opposition to such an office by Emperor Franz and, after his death, the probable rejection of a *major domus* by the court and especially by the senior archdukes. Any attempt to establish such an office would almost certainly have involved a violent power struggle.

Yet there was one moment when Metternich seemed to have attained supreme power without such a struggle. That was the moment of Emperor Franz's death when the political testament that the chancellor had so carefully helped to prepare came into force. Metternich was fully prepared to exercise supreme power. However, despite the powerful weapon of the testament, Metternich's authority collapsed abjectly as soon as Kolowrat challenged and defied it.

Why did Metternich avoid confrontations so anxiously and, when he could not evade a determined opponent, fail so miserably? Princess Melanie wrote in 1840 that during the struggle for internal reform a "frightful disgust overwhelmed him. He despises the meanness [of his opponents

[16] Walter, "Metternich-Gervay Briefwechsel", 230-37.

[17] Frankl, *Erinnerungen*, 224.

[18] Hübner, *Ein Jahr*, 13.

[19] See above, p. 115.

guided by] personal motives and egotism" [20]. This, while true, does not get us very far. Nor does Grillparzer's somewhat spiteful remark help that Metternich was trained "in diplomatic salons among women and courtiers, more polished than tempered, scratching with the tip instead of ripping with the edge" [21].

All his more discerning contemporaries noticed a fundamental weakness in Metternich that the Russian minister called "a basis of softness (un fond de mollesse) in his character" [22]. François Guizot pointed out that the quality Metternich lacked most was "courage, I mean the courage of impulse and of venture. He did not delight in fighting, and dreaded the perils more than he longed for the success he might attain" [23]. The Bavarian minister saw in him "something weak, unstable and changing ... that does not permit him ... to defeat a persistent opposition" [24]. Tsar Alexander I considered him

> no doubt a man of great intelligence, but the moment he sees the slightest difficulty, he hesitates, stops, looks all around for a way to escape, and then if he considers that he can no longer avoid this obstacle, he plants all his friends down in front of it [25].

"There was nothing creative in his character", Dr. Jäger, who had known Metternich for many years, remembered. "He could not give himself any impulses because he lacked the moral quality of being able to sacrifice himself" [26]. The French ambassador took up the Richelieu theme but found that the chancellor lacked some of the great as well as some of the bad qualities of the cardinal, particularly "that powerful will which, relying on itself, overturns the obstacles created by its ideas and drags them along in its wake" [27]. Henry Kissinger sums up this deficiency as the inability "to contemplate an abyss, not with the detachment of a scientist, but as a challenge to overcome – or to perish in the process" [28].

[20] *NP*, VI, 368.

[21] Grillparzer, *Sämtliche Werke*, part XV, 103.

[22] Meyendorff, "Portraits", 299.

[23] François Guizot, *Mémoirs pour servir à l'histoire de mon temps* (Paris: Michel Lévy Frères, 1858-67), IV, 22.

[24] Maximilian von Montgelas, *Denkwürdigkeiten (1799-1817)* (Stuttgart: Cotta'sche Buchhandlung, 1887), 394.

[25] Quoted in Guillaume de Bertier de Sauvigny, *Metternich et son temps* (Paris: La Librairie Hachette, 1959), 306.

[26] Frankl, *Erinnerungen*, 227, 224.

[27] Sainte-Aulaire, "Souvenirs" XXXI (September), 39f.

[28] Henry A. Kissinger, *A World Restored* (New York: Grosset & Dunlap, 1964), 322.

Gentz said of Metternich: "He is the only man ... who never felt remorse or regret at even the most obvious errors. Whenever he fails, he blames others or the circumstances" [29]. Srbik called this his "grotesque belief in his own infallibility" [30]. Princess Melanie noted with a rare tone of disapproval, "Clemens believes he can convince even the opponents" of internal reform [31]. In a chapter entitled "The cult of self", Bertier de Sauvigny, using Metternich's own words, illustrated his vanity and arrogance, and attributes them not to a continuous pose designed to assert his will, but to a subconscious awareness of his own deficiencies. The chancellor's boasting, Bertier de Sauvigny argues plausibly, "represents a kind of compensation" for the absence of real firmness and boldness [32].

If Metternich's stature as a statesman was limited because he lacked the ruthless determination and total commitment of a Napoleon or a Bismarck, it may also have been a consequence of his political ideology. He was a conservative whose "point of departure is order" [33], whose purpose was to conserve and maintain that order, and to permit change and progress only if it was "well-considered, imposed by the time, conforming to justice and fairness on all sides" [34].

He seemed to know his limitations from the beginning but blamed them on the time, a time out of joint which he felt called upon not to set right but to mitigate its excesses. "I ask myself daily", he wrote in 1823, "why providence let me be born too soon or too late". Three years earlier, at the age of forty-seven, he had been even more explicit.

> My life has fallen in an abominable period. I have been born either too soon or too late; now I do not feel good for anything. Earlier I would have relished the times, later I would have served to rebuild; today I spend my life shoring up decaying edifices. I should have been born in the year 1900 and have the twentieth century ahead of me [35].

[29] Prokesch-Osten, *Tagebücher*, 89. In London, in 1848, Metternich told his fellow exile Guizot: "Error has never come near my spirit". (Guizot, *Mémoirs*, IV, 21).

[30] Srbik, *Metternich*, III, 91.

[31] *NP*, VI, 226.

[32] Bertier de Sauvigny, *Metternich et son temps*, 14-24.

[33] *NP*, VII, 633.

[34] *NP*, VII, 33.

[35] *NP*, IV, 26; III, 348.

BIBLIOGRAPHICAL ESSAY

The Haus-, Hof- und Staatsarchiv in Vienna contains Metternich's reform plans and similar proposals by his contemporaries, as well as notes and reports (Vorträge) by Metternich and others, often with comments by the emperor. Unfortunately the Staatsrat Präsidium documents for the late 1820s and early 1830s have been destroyed during World War II. There are also important letters by Metternich, Kolowrat, Clam-Martinitz and Archduke Ludwig dealing with various aspects of internal reform, including the cabinet crisis of 1836. Only a few of these documents have been published. Friedrich Walter's collection *Die oesterreichische Zentralverwaltung, 1792-1848* (*Aktenstücke*) prints several of the more important ones. Hanns Schlitter's *Aus Oesterreichs Vormärz*, vol. IV also contains a few.

The eight volumes of Metternich's *Nachgelassene Papiere* offer a selected variety of important and useful documents, letters and memoirs, as well as extracts from Princess Melanie Metternich's diaries, but must be treated with caution. Metternich's bias and his editor's deletions – often without indication – have to be taken into account. Despite this limitation, however, there is a wealth of material in these volumes, not otherwise easily available, illustrating the chancellor's political principles and activities, personal attitudes and moods.

Archduke Johann's unpublished Tagebücher in the Landesarchiv, Graz, are very helpful because he was an acute observer of the political scene. His absence from Vienna usually promoted an objective point of view that broke down, however, when he wrote about Metternich or Metternich's enemies. Unfortunately here, too, World War II caused irreparable damage. The diaries covering his crucial role in the 1836 crisis have been destroyed.

The *Tagebücher* of Carl Kübeck, a highly efficient and honest administrator and statesman who rose from the son of a tailor to become Hofkammerpräsident and, after 1851, President of the Reichsrat, are a veritable goldmine for the first part of the century, particularly for the decade of the eighteen thirties. They provide penetrating and often caustic comments on contemporary events and personalities which bring the period to life. An additional volume of correspondence with Metternich is also valuable.

Wertheimer's long article "Fürst Metternich und die Staatskonferenz" is based on, and often quotes, the unpublished diaries of Count Heinrich Bombelles who had close connections with the court. Egon Corti stresses the importance of women in Metternich's private and political life and prints many otherwise unavailable letters in his *Metternich und die Frauen.* Metternich's *Lettres* to Countess Lieven afford a rare glimpse of his private thoughts and feelings.

Count Franz Hartig's *Genesis der Revolution in Oesterreich* is an indispensable book that analyzes and condemns the methods and structure of the Austrian government with a discerning insight based on his experience as a high civil servant and section head in the Staatsrat.

The older histories of the first half of the nineteenth century (Springer's *Geschichte Oesterreichs seit dem Wiener Frieden 1809* and Wertheimer's *Geschichte Oesterreichs und Ungarns im ersten Jahrzehnt des 19. Jahrhunderts*) are out of date. While containing many valuable things, their mistakes and omissions make them unreliable.

Easily the best history is *The Habsburg Empire, 1790-1918* by C.A. Macartney. He dismisses, however, surprisingly and incomprehensibly, the entire constitutional crisis of 1836 as of "little historic importance". A.J.P. Taylor in *The Habsburg Monarchy 1809-1918* and even more Hugo Hantsch in *Die Geschichte Oesterreichs* treat the period too superficially, concentrating on analysis to the virtual exclusion of facts. Hantsch is more sound, Taylor more readable. Erich Zöllner's *Geschichte Oesterreichs* is more factual but even more compressed. Friedrich Walter gives a generally helpful if disjointed account of the confusing structure of the Austrian government in his *Die Oesterreichische Zentralverwaltung 1792-1848.* The most penetrating examination of Austria's political and dynastic problems is *Das oesterreichische Staats- und Reichsproblem* by Joseph Redlich. Although it concentrates on the period 1848-67, its early chapters provide a helpful background for the first half of the century.

The range of Heinrich von Srbik's monumental biography *Metternich, der Staatsmann und der Mensch* includes much of the history of the time. His analysis of the chancellor's political thinking and "system" has been criticized for presenting it as too systematic a philosophy, but it is still a most valuable guide to Metternich's assumptions and premises.

Of more recent general books on Metternich, the most interesting and the only one to add something to Srbik is the psychological treatment of a complex personality in Bertier de Sauvigny's *Metternich et son temps*. Bibl's books are marred by his anti-Srbik polemics and his contempt for his subject. Except for some useful source material, they cannot be taken seriously as scholarly works.

BIBLIOGRAPHY

UNPUBLISHED PRIMARY SOURCES

Haus-, Hof- und Staatsarchiv, Vienna.
Kabinettarchiv, Konferenzakten, 1829, 1835.
Kaiser Franz Akten, Fasz. 41, 81.
Konferenz Akten S, 1846.
Minister Kolowrat Akten, 1835.
Staatskanzlei, Korrespondenz, Fasz. 91.
Staatskanzlei, Personalia, Metternich, Fasz. 12.
Staatsrat Präsidium (Organisierung und Instruktionen), Fasz. III, Kart. 3, 4.
Steiermarkisches Landesarchiv, Graz.
Erzherzog Johann, Tagebücher.

PUBLISHED PRIMARY SOURCES

Carl, Erzherzog. *Ausgewählte Schriften.* [Edited by F.X. Malcher]. 6 vols. Vienna: Braumüller, 1894.

Castle, Eduard. "Aus dem Tagebuch des Freiherrn Max von Löwenthal", *Historische Blätter,* I (1921/23), 495-512.

Chroust, Anton (ed.). *Gesandschaftsberichte aus München 1814-48.* Part I, vol. II. Munich: Kommission für bayerische Landesgeschichte, 1935.

Ficquelmont, L[udwig] von. *Aufklärungen.* Leipzig: Barth, 1850.

Frankl, Ludwig August. *Erinnerungen.* Edited by Stefan Hock. Prague: Josef Koch, 1910.

Grillparzer, Franz. *Sämtliche Werke.* Edited by Moritz Necker. 4 vols. (16 parts). Leipzig: Hesse & Becker, n.d.

Guizot, François. *Mémoirs pour servir à l'histoire de mon temps.* 8 vols. Paris: Michel Lévy Frères, 1861.

Hammer-Purgstall, Josef von. *Erinnerungen aus meinem Leben 1774-1852.* Edited by R. Bachofen von Echt. Vol. LXX of *Fontes Rerum Austriacarum.* Vienna: Hölder-Pichler-Tempsky, 1940.

Hübner, Alexander von. *Ein Jahr meines Lebens 1848-49.* Leipzig: Brockhaus, 1891.

Kübeck, Carl Friedrich von. *Tagebücher des Carl Friedrich Freiherrn von Kübeck von Kübau.* Edited by Max von Kübeck. 3 vols. Vienna: Gerold, 1909.

Metternich, Clemens Lothar von. *Aus Metternichs nachgelassenen Papieren.* Edited by Alfons von Klinkowström and Richard von Metternich. 8 vols. Vienna: Braumüller, 1880-84.

—, *Lettres du Prince de Metternich à la Comtesse de Lieven 1818-19.* Edited by Jean Hanoteau. Paris: Libraire Plon, 1909.

—, *Metternich-Hartig, ein Briefwechsel.* Edited by Franz Hartig. Vienna: Wiener Literarische Anstalt, 1923.

—, *Metternich und Kübeck. Ein Briefwechsel.* Edited by Max von Kübeck. Vienna: Gerold, 1910.

Meyendorff, Peter. "Portraits", *Baltische Monatsschrift*, LXX, Bd. 11 (1910), 289-304.

Montgelas, Maximilian von. *Denkwürdigkeiten (1799-1817).* Stuttgart: Cotta'sche Buchhandlung, 1887.

Prokesch von Osten, Anton. *Aus den Tagebüchern 1830-34.* Vienna: C. Reissers Söhne, 1909.

Sainte-Aulaire, Louis de. "Souvenirs de mon Ambassade à Vienne", *La Revue de Paris*, XXXI (1924), September, 1-42; December, 783-809.

—, *Souvenirs (Vienne, 1832-41).* Paris: Calman-Lévy, 1926.

Sambuy, Balbo Bertone di. *La Politica Estera del Piemonte sotto Carlo Alberto.* Edited by Mario degli Alberti. 3 vols. Turin: Fratelli Bocca Librai, 1913-19.

Walter, Friedrich. "Metternich und Gervay, ein Briefwechsel", *Mitteilungen des oesterreichischen Staatsarchivs*, IX (1956), 186-262.

—, (ed.). *Die oesterreichische Zentralverwaltung 1760-80. Aktenstücke.* Vienna: Holzhausens Nf., 1934.

—, (ed.). *Die oesterreichische Zentralverwaltung, 1792-1848. Aktenstücke.* Vienna: Holzhausens Nf., 1956.

CONTEMPORANEOUS POLITICAL LITERATURE

[Andrian-Werburg, Victor von]. *Oesterreich und dessen Zukunft.* 3rd ed. Hamburg: Hoffmann & Campe, 1843.

[Hartig, Franz von]. *Genesis der Revolution in Oesterreich im Jahre 1848.* Leipzig: Fleischer, 1850.

Müller, Adam von. *Gesammelte Schriften.* Munich: G. Franz, 1839.

SECONDARY SOURCES

Amburger, Eric. *Geschichte der Behördenorganisation Russlands von Peter dem Grossen bis 1917.* Leiden: E.J. Brill, 1966.

Beer, Adolf. *Die Finanzen Oesterreichs im 19. Jahrhundert.* Prague: Tempsky, 1877.

—, "Kübeck und Metternich", *Denkschriften der kaiserlichen Akademie der Wissenschaften*, XLV (1897), 1-157.

Beidtel, Ignaz. *Geschichte der oesterreichischen Staatsverwaltung 1740-1848.* Edited by Alfons Huber. 2 vols. Innsbruck: Wagner'sche Universitätsbuchhandlung, 1898.

Bertier de Sauvigny, Guillaume de. *Metternich et son temps*. Paris: La Librairie Hachette, 1959.

Bibl, Victor. *Kaiser Franz*. Leipzig: Johannes Günther, 1938.

—, *Metternich, der Dämon Oesterreichs*. Leipzig: Johannes Günther, 1936.

—, *Metternich in neuer Beleuchtung*. Vienna: L.W. Seidel, 1928.

—, *Die niederoesterreichischen Stände im Vormärz*. Vienna: Gerlach & Wiedling, 1911.

—, *Der Zerfall Oesterreichs*. 2 vols. Vienna: Rikola, 1922-24.

Büdinger, Max. "Zu den Verwaltungsgrundsätzen des Kaisers Franz", *Oesterreichisch-Ungarische Revue*, IV (1888), 257-84.

Corti, Egon Cäsar. *Metternich und die Frauen*. 2 vols. Zurich-Vienna: Europa Verlag, 1948.

Craig, Gordon A. *War, Politics and Diplomacy*. New York: Praeger, 1966.

Criste, Oskar. *Erzherzog Carl von Oesterreich*. 3 vols. Vienna: Braumüller, 1912.

Dahlman-Waitz. *Quellenkunde der Deutschen Geschichte*. 2 vols. 9th ed. Leipzig: K.F. Koehler, 1931.

Deslandres, Maurice. *Histoire constitutionelle de la France*. Vol. I. Paris: Librairie Armand Colin, 1932.

Durand, Charles. *Études sur le conseil d'état Napoléonien*. Paris: Presses Universitaires de France, 1949.

Engel-Janosi, Friedrich. "Zur Genesis der Revolution von 1848", *Zeitschrift für öffentliches Recht*, III (1922-23), 571-82.

Florinsky, Michael T. *Russia, a History and an Interpretation*. 2 vols. New York: Macmillan, 1964.

Fournier, August. "Graf Kolowrat und die oesterreichische Staatskonferenz von 1836", *Historische Studien und Skizzen*. 3. Reihe. Vienna: Tempsky, 1912.

Friedjung, Heinrich. *Oesterreich von 1848 bis 1860*. 2 vols. Stuttgart: Cotta'sche Buchhandlung Nf., 1908.

Grunwald, Constantin de. *Metternich*. London: Falcon Press, 1953.

Haas, Arthur G. *Metternich, Reorganization and Nationality 1813-1818*. Wiesbaden: Franz Steiner, 1963.

Hantsch, Hugo. *Die Geschichte Oesterreichs*. 4th ed. 2 vols. Graz: Styria, 1959.

Hintze, Otto. "Die Entstehung der modernen Staatsministerien", *Historische Zeitschrift*, C (1908), 53-111.

Hock, Carl von and Bidermann, Herman. *Der oesterreichische Staatsrat (1760-1848)*. Vienna: Braumüller, 1879.

Huber, Alfons. *Oesterreichische Reichsgeschichte*. Edited by Alfons Dopsch. Vienna: Tempsky, 1901.

Kann, Robert A. *Das Nationalitätenproblem der Habsburgermonarchie*. 2d ed. 2 vols. Graz-Cologne: H. Böhlaus Nf., 1964.

—, *A Study in Austrian Intellectual History*. New York: Praeger, 1960.

Kissinger, Henry A. *A World Restored*. New York: The Universal Library, 1964.

Kittel, E. "Metternichs politische Grundanschauungen", *Historische Vierteljahrschrift*, XXIV (1927), 443-83.

Krones, Franz von. "Freiherr von Baldacci über die inneren Zustände Oesterreichs", *Archiv für oesterreichische Geschichte*, LXXIV (1889), 1-160.

—, *Zur Geschichte Oesterreichs im Zeitalter der französischen Kriege und der Restauration, 1792 bis 1816*. Gotha: F.A. Perthes, 1886.

Langsam, Walter C. *Francis the Good.* New York, Macmillan, 1949.

Lefebvre, Georges. *Napoléon.* 3rd ed. Paris: Presses Universitaires de France, 1947.

Lehmann, Max. *Freiherr vom Stein.* 3 vols. Leipzig: S. Hirzel, 1902.

Maas, Ferdinand. *Der Josephinismus.* 5 vols. Vienna: Gerold, 1961.

Macartney, C.A. *The Habsburg Empire 1790-1918.* London: Weidenfeld & Nicolson, 1968.

Madelin, Louis. *The Consulate and the Empire.* Translated by E.F. Buckley. New York: Putnam's Sons, 1934.

Mayr, Josef Karl. *Geschichte der oesterreichischen Staatskanzlei im Zeitalter des Fürsten Metternich.* Vienna: Holzhausens Nf., 1935.

Meier, Ernst. *Französische Einflüsse auf die Staats- und Rechtentwicklung Preussens im XIX Jahrhundert.* Leipzig: Dunker & Humblot, 1908.

—, *Die Reform der Verwaltungsorganisation unter Stein und Hardenberg.* Leipzig: Dunker & Humblot, 1881.

Meynert, Hermann. *Kaiser Franz I: zur Geschichte seiner Regierung und seiner Zeit.* Vienna: Hölder, 1872.

Nolde, Boris. "L'autocratie Russe et la doctrine de la séparation des pouvoirs dans la première moitié du XIXe siècle", *Revue du Droit Public*, XLI (1924), 5-41.

Posch, Andreas. "Erzherzog Johann und Metternich", *Festschrift Julius Franz Schütz.* Edited by Berthold Sutter. Graz-Cologne: Böhlaus Nf., 1954.

Raeff, Marc. *Michael Speransky.* The Hague: Martinus Nijhoff, 1957.

Redlich, Joseph. *Das oesterreichische Staats- und Reichsproblem.* 2 vols. Leipzig: Der neue Geist Verlag, 1920.

Reinöhl, Fritz von. "Das politische Vermächtnis des Kaisers Franz I", *Historische Blätter*, 7. Heft (1937), 71-78.

Ritter, Gerhard. *Stein, eine politische Biographie.* 2 vols. Stuttgart: Deutsche Verlags-Anstalt, 1931.

Rothenberg, Gunther E. "The Austrian Army in the Age of Metternich", *Journal of Modern History*, XL (1968), 155-165.

Schiemann, Theodor. *Geschichte Russlands unter Kaiser Nikolaus I.* 4 vols. Berlin: Reimer, 1913.

Schlitter, Hanns. *Aus Oesterreichs Vormärz.* 4 vols. Vienna: Amalthea Verlag, 1920.

Schmidt, Adolf. *Zeitgenössige Geschichte.* Berlin: Dunker & Humblot, 1859.

Seeley, J.R. *Life and Times of Stein.* Cambridge: University Press, 1878.

Simon, Walter M. *The Failure of the Prussian Reform Movement 1807-1819.* Ithaca, N.Y.: Cornell University Press, 1955.

Spahn, Martin. "Metternich", *Hochland*, 6. Jahrgang, vol. II (1909), 154-73.

Springer, Anton. *Geschichte Oesterreichs seit dem Wiener Frieden 1809.* 2 vols. Leipzig: Hirzel, 1865.

Srbik, Heinrich von. "Der Ideengehalt des Metternichschen System", *Historische Zeitschrift*, CXXXI (1925), 240-62.

—, *Metternich: Der Staatsmann und der Mensch.* 3rd ed. 3 vols. Munich: Bruckmann, 1957.

Stern, Alfred. "L'idée d'une representation centrale de l'Autriche conçue par le Prince de Metternich", *Revue Historique*, XXXI (1886), 313-26.

Sutter, Berthold. "Erzherzog Johanns Kritik an Oesterreich", *Mitteilungen des oesterreichischen Staatsarchivs*, XVI (1963), 165-215.

Sybel, Heinrich von. "Die oesterreichische Staatskonferenz von 1836", *Kleine Historische Schriften*. Stuttgart: Cotta'sche Buchhandlung, 1880.

Taylor, A.J.P. *The Habsburg Monarchy 1809-1918*. London: Hamish Hamilton, 1948.

Valjavec, Fritz. *Der Josephinismus*. 2nd ed. Vienna: Verlag für Geschichte, 1945.

Walter Friedrich. "Franz Anton Graf Kolowrat-Liebsteinsky", *Neue oesterreichische Biographie ab 1815*. Vol. XV. Vienna: Amalthea-Verlag, 1963.

—, *Die oesterreichische Zentralverwaltung, 1740-80*. Vienna: Holzhausens Nf., 1938.

—, *Die oesterreichische Zentralverwaltung, 1792-1848*. Vienna: Holzhausens Nf., 1956.

—, "Der Rücktritt Graf Karl Choteks vom Oberstburggrafenamte und die Ernennung Erzherzog Stephans zum Landeschef in Böhmen", *Mitteilungen des Vereins für Geschichte der Deutschen in Böhmen*, LX (1922), 169-220.

Wandruszka, Adam. *The House of Habsburg*. New York: Anchor Books, 1964.

Wertheimer, Eduard. "Clam-Martinitz", *Allgemeine Deutsche Biographie, Nachträge*, XLIII (1903), 490-96.

—, "Fürst Metternich und die Staatskonferenz", *Oesterreichische Rundschau*, X (1907), 41-54, 111-128.

—, *Geschichte Oesterreichs und Ungarns im ersten Jahrzehnt des 19. Jahrhunderts*. 2 vols. Leipzig: Dunker & Humblot, 1884-90.

Wolfsgruber, Cölestin. *Franz I, Kaiser von Oesterreich*. 2 vols. Vienna: Braumüller, 1899.

Woodward, E.L. *Three Studies in European Conservatism*. London: Constable, 1929.

Wurzbach, Constant von. *Biographisches Lexikon des Kaisertums Oesterreich*. 60 vols. Vienna: Hof- und Staatsdruckerei, 1857-91.

Uhlirz, Karl. *Handbuch der Geschichte Oesterreichs und seiner Nachbarländer Böhmen und Ungarn*, vol. II, part 1. Graz: Leuschner & Lubensky, 1930,

Zöllner, Erich. *Geschichte Oesterreichs*. Vienna: Verlag für Geschichte und Politik. 1961.

INDEX

GPSR Compliance

The European Union's (EU) General Product Safety Regulation (GPSR) is a set of rules that requires consumer products to be safe and our obligations to ensure this.

If you have any concerns about our products, you can contact us on ProductSafety@springernature.com

In case Publisher is established outside the EU, the EU authorized representative is:

Springer Nature Customer Service Center GmbH
Europaplatz 3
69115 Heidelberg, Germany

Batch number: 10830943

Printed by Printforce, the Netherlands